W9-AAX-760

CREATIVE
PAPER
FOLDING

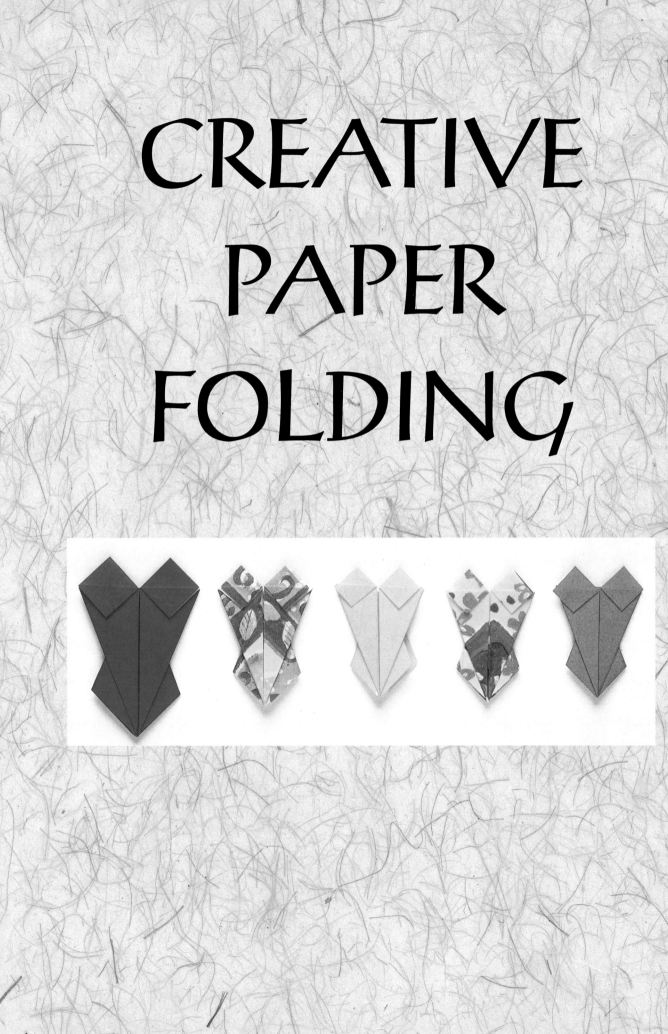

CREATIVE
PAPER
FOLDING

Mickey Baskett

Sterling Publishing Co., Inc.
New York

PROLIFIC IMPRESSIONS PRODUCTION STAFF:

Editor: Mickey Baskett
Copy: Sylvia Carroll
Graphics: Dianne Miller, Karen Turpin
Styling: Lenos Wallace
Photography: Jerry Mucklow, Pat Molnar
Administration: Jim Baskett

DESIGNERS:

Patty Cox   Susan S. Mickey   Lani Temple
Lisa Koo   Ellen Ishino Rankart

ACKNOWLEDGEMENTS

Designers would like to thank the following companies for their generosity in supplying materials for the projects in this book:

Papers by Catherine
11328 s. Post Oak Rd.
Suite 108
Houston, TX 77035
vellum paper supplier

Canson-Talens
21 Industrial Dr.
S. Hadley, MA 01075
vellum paper supplier

Design Originals
2425 Cullen St.
Ft. Worth, TX 76107
Tea bag folding paper supplier

CM Offray & Son, Inc.
Rt. 24, Box 601
Chester, NJ 07930
ribbon supplier

Forster, Inc.
P.O. Box 657
Wilton, ME 04294
supplier of small wooden findings, dowels

Library of Congress Cataloging-in-Publication Data Available

Baskett, Mickey.
    Creative paper folding / Mickey Baskett.
        p. cm.
    ISBN 0-8069-2751-8
        1. Paper work. I. Title.

TT870.B244 2000
736'.98-dc21

00-058314

First paperback edition published in 2002 by
Sterling Publishing Company, Inc.
387 Park Avenue South, New York, N.Y. 10016
Produced by Prolific Impressions, Inc.
160 South Candler St., Decatur, GA 30030
Distributed in Canada by Sterling Publishing
c/o Canadian Manda Group, One Atlantic Avenue, Suite 105
Toronto, Ontario, Canada M6K 3E7
Distributed in Great Britain and Europe by Cassell PLC
Wellington House, 125 Strand, London WC2R 0BB, England
Distributed in Australia by Capricorn Link (Australia) Pty. Ltd.
P.O. Box 704, Windsor, NSW 2756 Australia

Printed in China
All rights reserved

Sterling ISBN 0-8069-2751-8 Hardcover
                0-8069-7545-8 Paperback

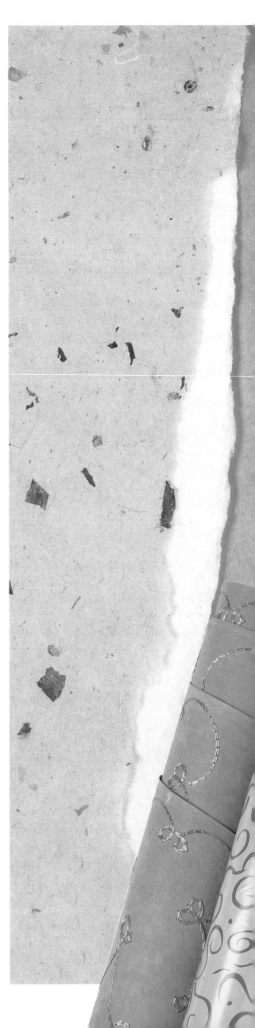

CONTENTS

PAPER FOLDING

A brief history of an ancient art made easy

Paper folding is often thought to be an invention of the Japanese as most people are familiar with *origami*. However, the Japanese merely gave a name to an art that has been practiced for centuries. In Japan, paper folding has reached its greatest development, with hundreds of traditional folds and an extensive literature. The art was named by the Japanese, *oru* meaning "to fold" and *kami* meaning "paper." (It was originally called *orukami*.)

Most authorities believe that paper folding began in China in the first century AD along with the invention of paper. The discovery is usually credited to Ts'ai Lun – a Chinese court official. Paper folding and paper making were kept secret by the Chinese for about 500 years, but eventually Buddhist monks took the practice to Japan. Japan has probably appreciated the art more than anyone and developed it tremendously with hundreds of traditional folds. The Japanese used it originally in Shinto religious rituals and ceremonial etiquette. Yoshizawa of Tokyo is considered

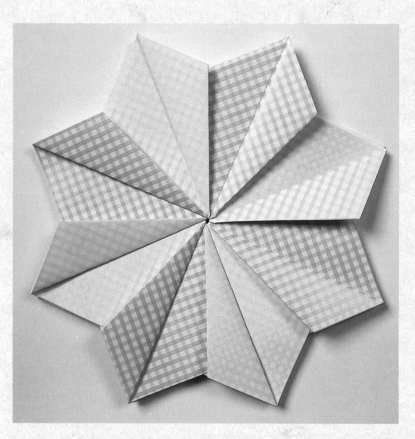

the greatest of modern paper folders. He wrote several books on origami and created a large number of new, often fantastically complex, figures possessing great realism and delicate beauty.

Paper folding spread from China to Arab nations in another way. In 751, the Arabs occupying Samarkland were attacked by China. In repelling the attack, several Chinese prisoners were taken who were skilled in paper making and paper folding. The art thus spread westward. It reached Egypt in the 10th Century.

In the 12th Century, the Moors established paper folding in Spain, and it reached Italy through the Arab occupation of Sicily. It quickly moved from Italy to the rest of Europe. Paper was used in England at the start of the 14th Century. From there it was brought to the Americas, with the first paper mill in North America being built in 1690 at Roxboro, PA. Wherever paper was introduced, the art of paper folding followed.

In Europe in the 16th Century, wonderful napkin folding was practiced. Many of these folds were incorporated into origami.

Apart from the Oriental tradition, the folding of colored papers into ornamental designs was introduced into the kindergarten movement in Germany in the 19th Century. Later a famous German school of design stressed paper folding in training students for commercial designs.

Paper folding also flourished in Spain and South America at the turn of the 20th century when Miguel de Unamuno, a Spanish writer and philosopher, made a hobby of the art and wrote a humorous essay on it. Vicente Solorzano Sagredo of Argentina wrote many comprehensive manuals of the art in Spanish.

Tea Bag Folding had an entirely different origin, beginning in Europe. As the story goes, a woman sipping a lovely cup of tea absent-mindedly picked up the empty tea bag or envelope jacket and began folding it. A few more folds turned into a star shape, and Tea Bag Folding had begun. Original European tea bags were printed with pretty patterns that made lovely little ornaments when folded.

In this book you will find a wide variety of things to make with folded paper, and a variety of paper types used. We hope you enjoy your paper folding and its resulting beauty. ❏

PAPER TYPES

Many types of paper can be used for your paper folding projects. The best choice depends on your project. Determine what paper qualities are most important for your project. Qualities to consider are: the weight of the paper -whether it needs to be lightweight or sturdy; flexibility of the paper; whether the paper holds a crease; color or design of paper; price of paper; and availability of paper. For instance, a box needs sturdy paper while a tree ornament needs to be made of lightweight paper. The large rose projects in this book work best with handmade or other flexible paper while the heart petal rose works best with tissue paper. The suncatchers work best with a translucent paper. The tea bag folded projects need a paper that will hold a crease and be lightweight.

Sources for papers to use are multiple. While you can use readily available papers such as giftwrap, be sure to explore places such as office supply stores, stationery stores, art supply shops, and craft outlets. The variety of papers available at these places are truly wonderful.

Following are some types of papers that you can use for paper folding projects:

◆ Stationery Papers

These papers are widely available in office supply stores and art stores everywhere. Stationery comes in different weights and colors. Three kinds most commonly found are "laid," "bond," and "woven." Bond is of good quality and takes repeated handling. Laid has tiny parallel lines running throughout and is perfect for photocopying and paper art projects. Woven is made of finely meshed fibers and has the look of fine fabric.

◆ Wrapping Paper

Widely available and versatile, almost any color and pattern is available. These papers are usually printed on one side and white on the backside. Be sure to consider this aspect for your folded project.

◆ Brown Kraft Paper

This paper is traditionally used for wrapping parcels and can be found in rolls or sheets. This versatile paper is inexpensive and can be used for a variety of paper crafting techniques. The color and texture makes it perfect for a natural look.

◆ Colored Art Papers

These are excellent for many paper art projects, especially paper folding and paper sculpture. They are fade-resistant and bleed-resistant. They are usually available in art supply stores in a variety of solid colors, 80 lb. weight, and in large 22" x 32" sheets.

◆ Canford Papers

These papers are acid-free and have a smooth, matte surface that accepts pencil, chalk, pastel, marker and crayon. In addition they are great for folding, quilling, cutting, or sculpture. These papers also glue and emboss well. They are also wonderful for screen printing, black printing, photocopying, and for use with bubble-jet or laser printers. This is a 70-lb. weight paper and usually found in large 20-1/2" x 30-1/2" sheets.

◆ Parchment

Traditionally parchment was made of animal skins. Today parchment paper refers to a strong, fine-textured paper that is translucent. Sometimes "vellum" and "parchment" are used interchangeably. Parchment paper usually has a mottled look that resembles the original look of the animal skin parchment. It is excellent for invitations, placecards, and home decor projects.

◆ Mi-Tientes Drawing Papers

This classic French paper has a "vellum" texture on the top side and a flat surface on the reverse. It is a heavy sheet (98-lb.) with a high rag content to ensure long life without deterioration.

◆ Origami Papers

There are many papers created especially for origami. Special origami papers are smooth-surfaced, hold a rigid crease, and usually are sold in pre-cut sizes. Some of these special origami papers are:

Aurora Iridescent Squares – smooth-surfaced iridescent sheets in 5-7/8" squares;

Large Origami Papers in a rainbow of bright colors on one side and white on the reverse side in 9" squares;

Metallic Squares – lightweight 6" squares in a variety of metallic colors on one side and white on the other;

Folk Art Squares – 6" and 4-5/8" squares with a variety of folk art patterns on one side;

Harmony Squares – 6" and 4-5/8" squares each using two colors on each sheet;

Double Sided Paper in assorted bright colors with a different color on each side.

◈ Glassine Paper

This is a sturdy, colored and mottled transparent paper. It folds and cuts nicely.

◈ Tissue Paper

Can be found in a variety of places, in solids and patterns. They are very light weight and translucent.

◈ Waxed Tissue Papers

These papers can be joined together with a warm iron rather than gluing. The wax also adds another dimension when wrinkled.

◈ Handmade and Decorative Papers

Everyone loves the look and feel of handmade paper. The papers are usually sturdy and flexible. They add a special quality to your folded projects that make them perfect for gifts. Following are some types of handmade paper that would be interesting for many of the paper projects in this book:

Barkpaper: This original paper of the Western Hemisphere is still made today as it was in the 1300s from the bark from downed fig and mulberry trees, washed in streams and boiled in lime water. The damp, pliable fibers are beaten, then laid out in the sun to dry. It's a beautiful primitive paper available in nine colors in 16" x 24" sheets.

Reciclados is a gray handmade paper speckled with purple ink and corn husk.

Egyptian Papyrus Paper is the oldest writing material in existence today, dating back at least 5,000 years. While it's not good for the smaller and more intricate folded designs, it would work well for a lampshade.

Lama Li Festive Papers: Handmade in Nepal from the fibers of the Lokta plant, these papers are decorated with hand silk-screened patterns of butterflies or flowers or with boddhi tree leaves embedded in the paper itself.

Garden Papers: These handmade, cotton-soft papers are adorned with rustic elements from the garden. No two sheets are alike.

◈ Embossed Papers

These thick, rugged papers are heavily textured with deeply embossed patterns. However, avoid these for the smaller, more intricate folded designs.

◈ Handscreened India Papers

These 35-lb. natural papers reflect the traditional patterns and colors commonly screen-printed on fabric in India. They are particularly good for the tea bag folded designs. Available in 22" x 30" sheets.

◈ Lace Paper

Japanese Lace Paper and White Lace Paper are elegant and wonderful for gift tags, luminaries, flowers, or a lamp. Thai Lace paper is machine-made from 100% kozo. It is graceful, extremely soft, and easy to work with.

◈ French Marble Papers

These beautiful ink marbleized papers are masterpieces on their own! Designs range from intricate combed designs to freeform patterns to exquisite designs. Patterns are only on one side and may vary from sheet to sheet.

◈ Corrugated Paper

This type of paper is great for boxes and gift cards. Brightly colored on one side and white on the other, it is rigid on the width and flexible on the length. It adds texture and dimension to projects. Available in 12" x 16" sheets or in 48" side x 25-ft. rolls. ❑

SUPPLIES

Following is a list of supplies you should have handy for all your paper folding projects. Depending upon the project you are making, you may need other supplies. Consult supply list of individual project instructions for additional supplies needed.

◈ Bone Folder

This tool, made with real bone, is a must for paper folding. It is a smooth-edged tool used for making precise folds in paper, burnishing creases, scoring paper, and embossing. It is especially invaluable when using fibrous and heavy papers.

◈ Ruler

Most of these projects require precise measurements and perfectly straight folds. Use your ruler for accurate measuring and folding.

◈ Cutting Tools

A variety of cutting tools can be used for cutting your paper to size and shape.

Knives: Art or craft knives or utility knives are probably best. Make sure you have plenty of sharp blades on hand and change blades when necessary. These knives are also used to score papers that are too heavy to be scored with the bone folder.

Scissors: Sharp, small scissors are sometimes needed for cutting small and curved shapes, such as for a snowflake. Scissors with decorative designs can cut a scalloped or other decorative edge, perfect for gift cards or envelopes. Pinking shears give a zigzag edge.

Circle Cutter: To cut circles easily and quickly, use a circle cutter. Just rest the cutter on paper to be cut, press the spring-action handle arm down and rotate around to cut a clean circle.

◈ Cutting Mat

You must protect your work surfaces from being marred when you cut. At the very least, cut your paper on a stack of newspapers. Better than that is a cutting board. And better still is a self- healing cutting mat. Cutting mats are available in several sizes. Some are translucent and some are also marked off in a grid.

◈ Tools for Drawing Shapes

When cutting or folding 90-degree angles, the way to insure absolutely straight and perpendicular lines and folds is to use a **T-square.** Likewise, use a **French curve** to assure properly drawn curves. When drawing a circle, use a **compass** for a perfect one of the exact size you desire. A **protractor** will enable you to measure and draw angles accurately. **Templates** of various sizes and shapes are also handy.

◈ Punching Tools

Hole Punch: These tools punch small circles or sometimes a diamond shape. Use this for some of the cutout design areas of the folded snowflake.

Corner Decorating Punches: With one punch, you can add a triplet of stars, flowers, asterisk-shapes or hearts in the corners of a paper or on scallops.

Corner Lace Punches: These punches are also for creating decorative corners or papers. They create professional die-cut shapes in a variety of styles and sizes that are easy to punch.

◈ Marking Tools

Pencils, pens, and markers will enable you to draw lines and mark measurements from light and erasable to clearly visible, as needed.

◈ Glue

White craft glue is used where papers need to be glued. If the area will be difficult to hold, thick white craft glue is used. A glue stick is also a handy gluing-tool and is perfect for some projects. Low-melt and hot glue sticks with a glue gun are sometimes used to attach embellishments such as dried florals.

◈ Paper Clips, Straight Pins & Push Pins

When some folds are glued, it is helpful to hold them in place with paper clips. In some cases, you may hold folds or folded parts in place with straight pins or push pins. The large rose, for instance, is made on a paper-covered plastic foam half-ball. Straight pins are perfect for holding the petals in place on the base while the glue dries.

◈ Two-Sided Tape

On several projects, parts are connected with two sided tape. For instance, some flowers are attached to their stem with double stick tape between the folds of the flower. It is also an option instead of gluing when securing the bottoms of folded giftbags.

◈ Clear Acrylic Spray Finish

This will help some finished projects hold a shape by stiffening the paper after design is formed.

How To Fold Papers

Pattern Markings

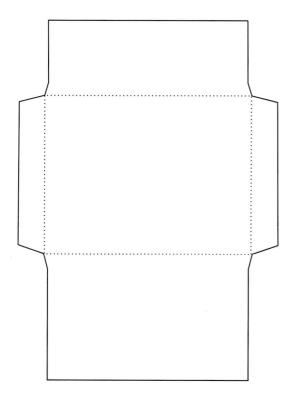

A dotted line on a pattern or diagram indicates a paper fold.

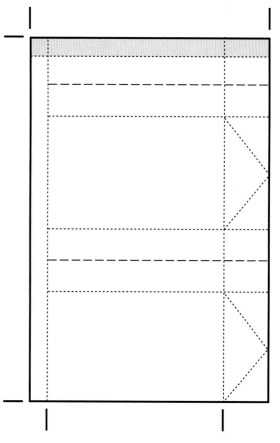

A dashed line indicates a fold in the opposite direction. Think of the dashed lines as valleys and the dotted lines as mountains.

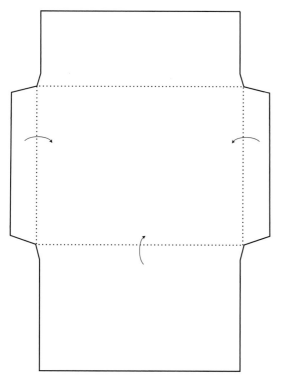

An arrow indicates the direction in which to make the fold.

An arrow with an arc indicates to turn the whole project in the other direction.

An arrow with a circle indicates to turn the entire project over.

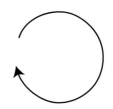

Proper Folding

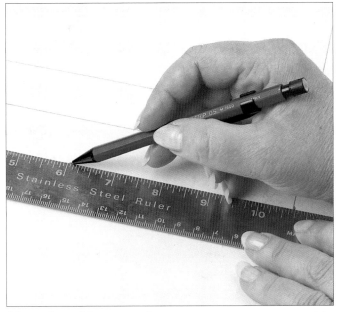

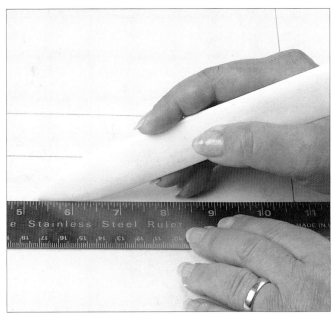

Measuring: Measure and cut your paper very accurately. Measure for your fold lines very accurately. This will affect your final results.

Straight Folds: Making perfectly straight folds is also important. To insure that they are straight, score the paper along a straight ruler edge using a bone folder.

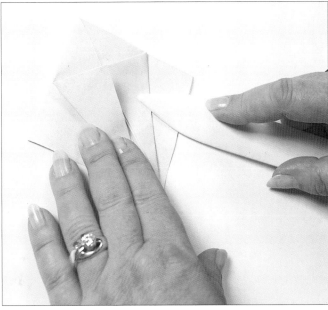

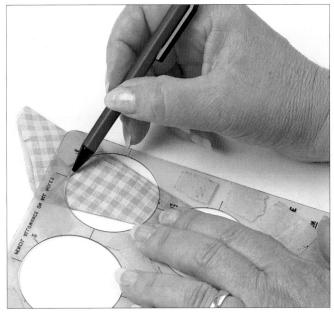

Creasing: When you make a fold, it should be creased. Burnish it with the bone folder for an excellent crease.

Using Templates: Templates, French curves, and protractors help to make perfectly straight curves, circles, and ovals. Use a pencil to draw the line, then use a craft knife to cut along line. If you use a craft knife to cut the line against the template, you run the risk of nicking the template and ruining the perfectly smooth curve.

Scoring: On some projects with heavier paper, the folds may need to be scored. The bone folder can also be used for scoring folds. For some projects made with cardboard, certain fold lines must be scored with a razor blade or craft knife. Use a straight edge to score exactly on the line. Be sure not to cut all the way through.

Reverse Folds: The term "reverse fold" is sometimes used. This means to fold along a previous fold line in the opposite direction from which it was originally folded. The term also sometimes means to fold in the opposite direction from surrounding folds. ❑

BAGS & BOXES

Gifts can be more special than ever by making your own giftbags and gift boxes. Giftbags can be sized perfectly for what they are to hold. Diagrams are given here for three sizes plus a wine bag, and directions also tell you how to measure for whatever size you want to make. Make giftbags from the same paper used to wrap other packages at Christmas for a coordinated theme. Choosing your own paper will allow you to make your bags fit the occasion.

The folded paper boxes can be made of paper so pretty that you won't need to wrap the gift – just tie a ribbon around it. These are also lovely enough to use in home decorating for holding small loose items. Making boxes of corrugated cardboard are easy to make and delightful to receive, adding a special touch to a gift. ❑

Giftbag Gaiety

*Designed by
Susan S. Mickey*

SUPPLIES

Paper: a sturdy, heavy paper works
best; however, wrapping paper
is also a choice.

Ruler

Hole punch

Two-sided tape or thick white glue

Cord or ribbon, 28" to 32"

Instructions follow on page 18

Giftbag Gaiety

Supplies on page 16

INSTRUCTIONS

1. Using the patterns on page 20 & 21 for the size bag you desire (use Figs 1, 2, 3, or 4), measure and mark this pattern onto the backside of the paper you have chosen to make the bag. Be sure to mark all the lines on the pattern onto your paper so you will know where to fold. See Photo 1. Width and height can be adjusted to other sizes and shapes you might desire, as follows. Double the desired width and add 7" (for two 3" sides and a 1" overlap) to obtain first measurement. Add 3-1/2" to 4" (for bottom and top "hem") to desired height to obtain second measurement. Measure and mark fold lines for front, back, sides, bottom, side overlap, and top "hem" on your paper.

2. Cut paper along the outside line to appropriate size. A metal straight edge and a craft knife is the best way to cut out your bag size.

3. Use the bone folder to score along the fold lines. This will make it easier to obtain a straight fold. See Photo 2.

4. Begin folding the bag. The dotted lines on diagrams represent "valley" folds – fold paper wrong side to wrong side. The dashed lines represent "mountain" folds – fold paper right side to right side. To begin, fold the top and bottom of the paper as shown on diagrams. Fold lines should be creased well and slightly scored with a folding bone, then creased with the folding bone. See Photo 3.

5. Using measurements on diagram (or your own adjusted measurements), make the vertical folds of bag to create the sides. You will have an overlap piece at the end of one side. Glue or tape (with double-side tape) to secure flap. See Photo 4.

6. Creating Bottom: Fold the diagonal lines to create the triangular flap at the bottom of bag back. Fold the bag back at right angles to the adjacent side. The bottom will begin to form. Tape or glue the flap to the bottom. Continue around the bag: Fold the diagonal lines to make the flap at bottom of bag front. Fold bag front and the next side at right angles. This will form the remainder of bottom. Tape or glue as you go, with the flaps on outside bottom. The points of the flaps will overlap each other. See Photo 5.

7. Handle: There are many methods of attaching handles. For instance, ends of cord or ribbon can simply be glued on the inside. Following is a very neat way: Punch two sets of holes on bag front and back opposite each other along the top "hem" fold. See Photo 6. Place a square of double stick tape (or some glue) on inside below each hole. Cut cord or ribbon in half for two handles. Thread the ends of cord or ribbon through the holes with ends on inside of bag. Fold the top "hem" back to inside onto the tape or glue, sandwiching and securing the ends of the cord between outside of bag and the "hem." ❑

Photo 1: Measure and draw bag pattern on backside of paper.

Photo 2: Score along fold lines to make it easier to obtain a straight fold.

Photo 3: Begin folding bag, creasing with bone folder.

Photo 5: Fold, crease, and secure bottom of bag.

Photo 4: Glue or tape side overlap of bag.

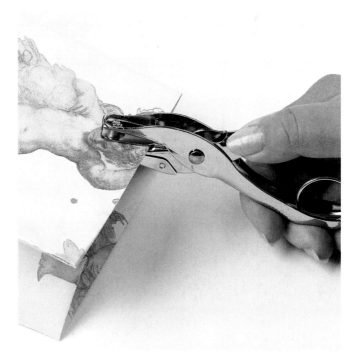

Photo 6: Punch holes at top of bag for attaching handles.

Giftbag Gaiety

Patterns for 4 sizes of giftbags

Fig. 1
Small Bag

Finished Size: 5" × 8"

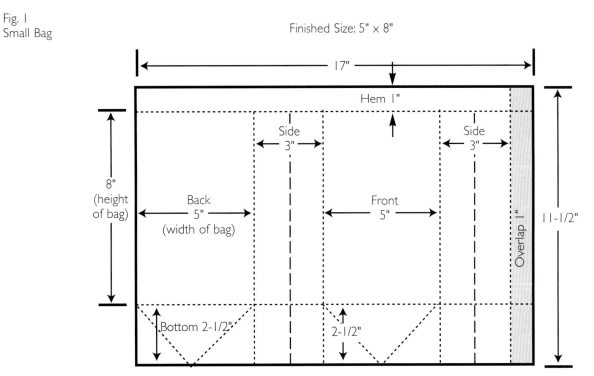

Fig. 2
Medium Bag

Finished Size: 6" × 10"

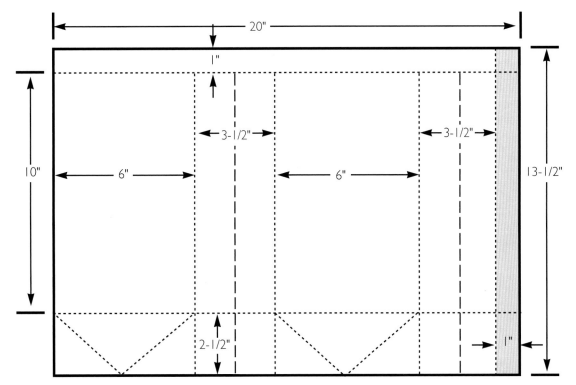

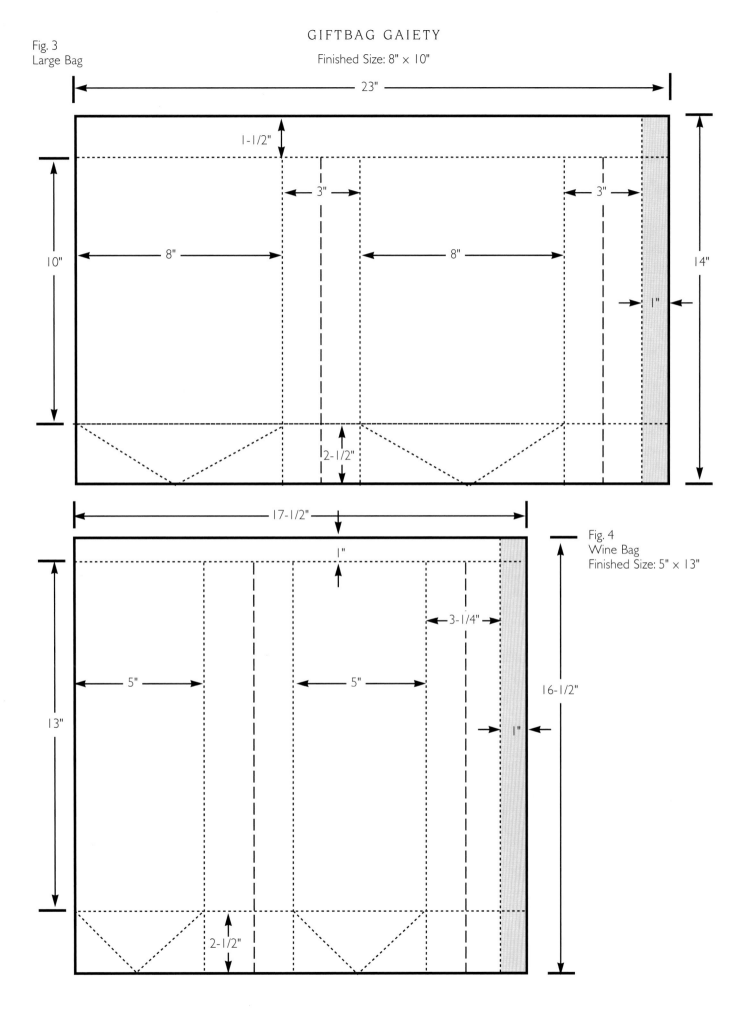

GIFTBAG GAIETY
Finished Size: 8" × 10"

Fig. 3
Large Bag

23"

1-1/2"

3"   3"

10"   8"   8"   14"

1"

2-1/2"

17-1/2"

1"

Fig. 4
Wine Bag
Finished Size: 5" × 13"

3-1/4"

5"   5"

16-1/2"

13"   1"

2-1/2"

Origami Boxes

Designed by Lisa Koo

SUPPLIES

Two squares of heavy weight paper per
box (3 sizes shown):
  Large (5-1/2" x 5-1/2" x 2-3/4"): 15"
    and 14-1/2" squares
  Medium (4-1/2" x 4-1/2" x 2-1/4"):
    13" and 12-1/2" squares
  Small (3" x 3" x 1-1/2"): 8" and 7-1/2"
    squares

INSTRUCTIONS

*Use the larger of the two squares for the
lid and the smaller for the box.*

1. Place paper on work surface wrong side
   up. Fold the four corners to the center
   (Fig. 1). Crease well.
2. Fold the top edge and bottom edge to
   center (Fig. 2). Crease well and unfold.
3. Fold the left edge and right edge to center (Fig. 3). Crease well and unfold.
4. Unfold the top and bottom triangles
   (Fig. 4).
5. Bring the corners of fold A and B
   together at top and bottom. While holding both A and B, bring corners C to
   outer points A and B at top and bottom
   (Fig. 5). This will create diagonal folds
   in corners as shown by dotted lines in
   Fig. 5.
6. Fold the pointed flaps over onto inside
   side and bottom of box.
7. Repeat with the other square for box
   lid.
8. Tie box with ribbon. ❏

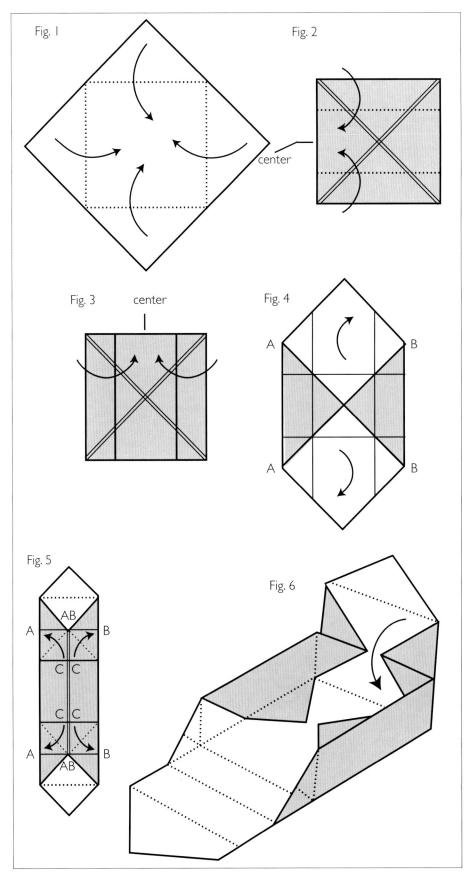

Shallow
Gift Boxes

Designed by
Susan S. Mickey

SUPPLIES

Cardboard (corrugated shown):
  Small (5" x 2-1/2" x 1"):
    9" x 10" piece
  Large (6-1/2" x 3-1/4" x
    1-1/4): 11-1/2" x 11-1/2"
    piece

Scissors or craft or utility knife

Thick white glue

Instructions follow on page 26

Shallow Gift Boxes

Supplies listed on page 24

INSTRUCTIONS

1. Draw a pattern for the gift box using the diagram for the size you wish (Fig. 1). Follow the measurements exactly. If you wish a different size, enlarge or reduce on a photo copier so measurements will be proportionate.

2. Cut out cardboard along the exterior lines of the pattern (Fig. 2), making cuts evenly and neatly.

3. On the right side of box (what will be outside), score the fold lines with your folding bone, scissors, or craft knife. Be care-ful not to cut all the way through.

4. At this time you can decorate the front edge of your box (such as with scallops) or decorate the surface.

5. Fold along the fold lines as indicated on the diagram, gluing the box together as you go (Fig. 3). First glue tabs to the inside of sides. Fold flaps to inside over tabs and glue in place.

6. Stuff with tissue paper and/or shredded paper before filling with a gift. Tie around box with a ribbon (Fig. 4). ❏

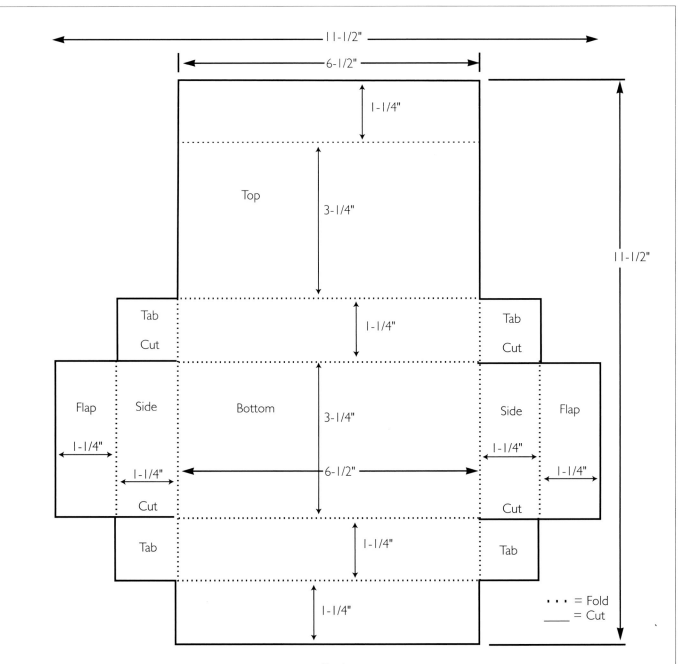

Fig. 1
Large Box
Finished Size: 6-1/2" x 3-1/4" x 1-1/4"

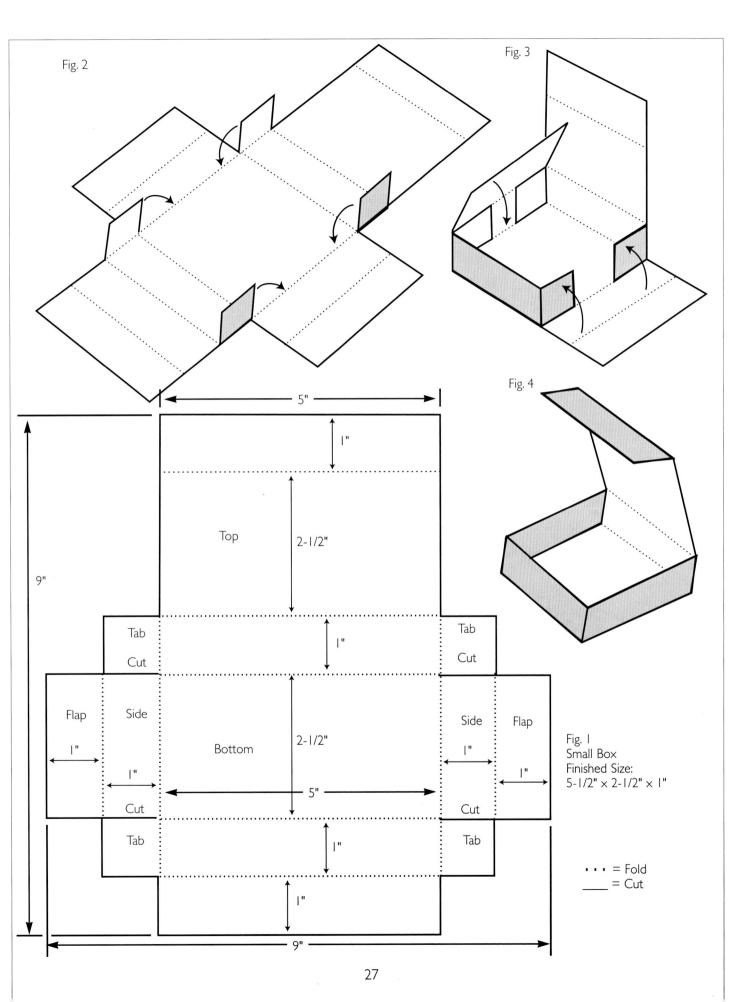

Fig. 2

Fig. 3

Fig. 4

5"

1"

Top

2-1/2"

1"

Tab | Tab
Cut | Cut

Flap | Side | | Side | Flap

1" | | | 1"

1" | | | 1"

Bottom | 2-1/2"

5"

Cut | Cut

Tab | Tab

1"

9"

1"

9"

Fig. 1
Small Box
Finished Size:
5-1/2" × 2-1/2" × 1"

• • • = Fold
_____ = Cut

CARDS
&
ENVELOPES

No greeting card can say "I care" more than one you made yourself. What's more, these card projects are beautiful, interesting, and unique.

The Tea Bag Folded Star Cards are fascinating. The look of the star can change from one kaleidoscopic design to another by just using a different patterned paper, and the folded star is as beautiful on the "back" as on the "front." For these card projects, both sides are displayed.

The folded kissing cranes can be used on card in a myriad of ways, and several ways are shown here. Simple folded pinwheels make beautiful adornments for cards. The heart card is a delight as it unfolds one side at a time.

Make your own envelopes, too, from pretty paper. There is a pattern and instructions for the usual square or rectangular envelope with suggestions for embellishments as well as patterns for unusual many-sided envelopes with scallops that tuck into each other.

Your greetings were never so grand!

Tea Bag Folded Star Greeting Cards

Designed by Lani Temple

The same folded star can look very different. When folded, the front shows a beautiful star and the back shows a lovely medallion. Either side can be displayed. On the cards shown, the folded motif is nestled in a circle so that one side of the folded star shows on the front of the card and the other side on the inside of the card. The star and medallion can also look very different with different paper designs. By attaching a ribbon hanger to the star, the recipient of the card can remove the folded star and use as an ornament.

Instructions on page 32

Tea Bag Folded Star Greeting Cards

SUPPLIES

Decorative paper, eight 2" squares

Colored card stock, 8-1/2" x 5-1/2"

Circle cutter

Decorative edge scissors

Ribbon

White craft glue

INSTRUCTIONS

for Making Star:

1. Fold each square diagonally both ways, then in half both ways. Unfold. See Fig. 1.

2. Fold the top corner down to meet the bottom corner to make a triangle. See Fig. 2.

3. Push the left and right corners inward, making two reverse folds. This brings the left and right corners down to the bottom corner so that all four corners meet at the bottom, forming a diamond. See Fig. 3.

4. Fold both side points of the upper layer to the center. Unfold. Fold the top down. Unfold. See Fig. 4

5. Separate the top layer and pull the bottom point up. The side points will pull in to center and meet. See Fig. 5.

6. Flatten the sides to form a long narrow diamond. (A small triangle will form under each side of the long narrow diamond. A "diagonal square" diamond will be at the bottom of the back, if turned over.) See Fig. 6.

7. Make eight of these and interlock them, slipping the left point of the bottom layer of one piece under the top layer of adjacent piece. Dot glue in folds to secure. See Fig. 7.

for Making Card:

1. Fold card stock in half to a 4-1/4" x 5-1/2" size, with fold on left side.

2. With circle cutter, cut a circle centered on front of card just the size of the design on backside of folded star.

3. Nestle folded design into hole so that one design shows on front of card and the other design (on back of folded piece) shows on inside of card.

4. If desired, cut card edges with decorative edged scissors and/or tie a ribbon around fold of card. ❑

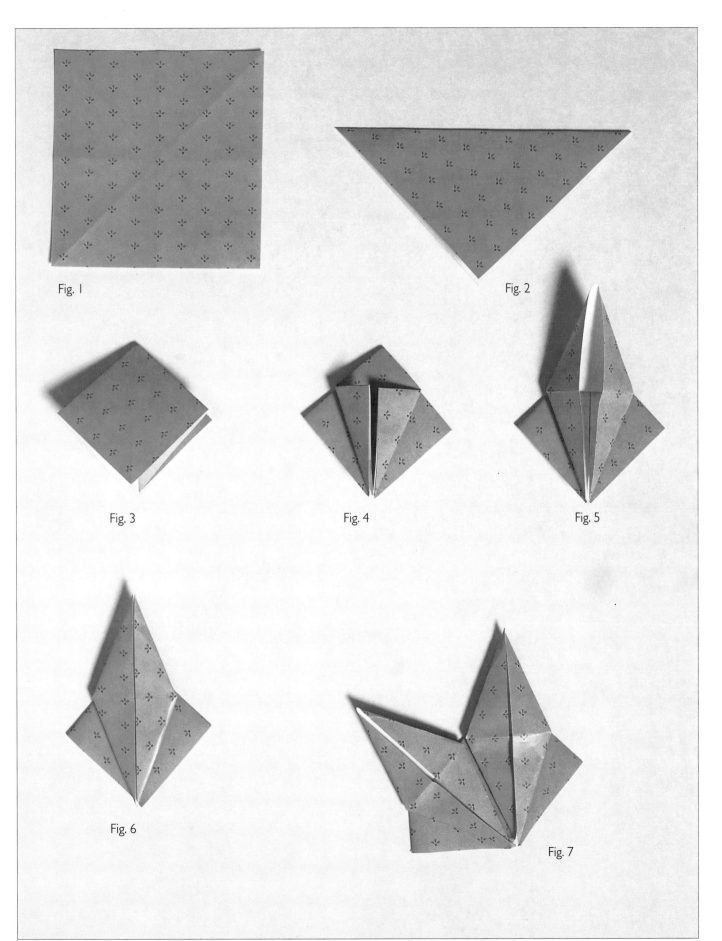

Fig. 1

Fig. 2

Fig. 3

Fig. 4

Fig. 5

Fig. 6

Fig. 7

Kissing Cranes Greeting Cards

Designed by Lisa Koo

SUPPLIES

Two 2" squares paper for cranes
Heavy paper or card stock for greeting
  card
White craft glue
Backing paper if card has a window on
  front

INSTRUCTIONS

for Making Cranes:

1. Place 2" x 2" paper on work surface wrong side up. Fold diagonally. Crease well and unfold. (Fig. 1)
2. Fold A-B edge and B-C edge to center crease, bringing A and C corners together at center crease. (Fig. 2)
3. This will form a kite shape (Fig. 3). Re-letter points as shown.
4. Fold to bring point A to point C (Fig. 4).
5. From point B, measure 1-1/2" along top edge and 1-7/8" along bottom edge. Use the line between these to points as a folding line. Fold up point B along this line to form the neck of bird (Fig. 5). Crease well.
6. On neck of bird, measure from point B 1/2" and 5/8" as shown. Use the line between these two points as a folding line and fold point B downward to form the beak of the bird (Fig. 6). Crease well.

When making second crane, make the folds in step 4 behind the paper instead of forward. This will make a mirror image of the first crane so they can be placed face to face.

for Making Card:

Fold paper for card in half. One card is shown with a top fold; two others are shown with a left side fold. If card is to have a window, cut it from front of card. (Shown is a heart shaped window and a 4-pane "window" window.) Glue backing paper inside card behind window. Glue cranes facing each other either on front of card or in window of card. Embellish with ribbon or painted border around window, as desired. ❑

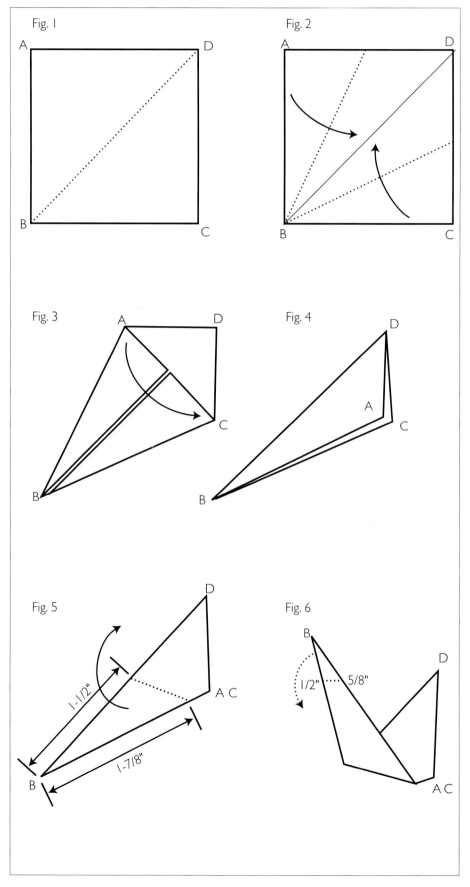

Fig. 1

Fig. 2

Fig. 3

Fig. 4

Fig. 5

Fig. 6

Flat Pinwheel Greeting Card

Designed by Lisa Koo

SUPPLIES

Paper for pinwheels, 2" square for each
Heavy paper or card stock for greeting card
Fine point permanent pen
White craft glue

INSTRUCTIONS

for Making Pinwheel:

1. Place 2" x 2" paper on work surface wrong side up. Fold diagonally (Fig. 1). Crease well and unfold.
2. Fold both sides to center (Fig. 2 & 3).
3. Fold top and bottom to center (Fig. 4).
4. Diagonally fold the lower corners of top half to top center (Fig. 5). Crease. Unfold.
5. Pulling on the underlayer of these triangles, pull them out to the sides as far as they go to create pointed flaps (Fig. 6). Crease.
6. Fold the left flap to point upward (Fig 7).
7. Rotate the paper 180-degrees and repeat steps 4-6 (Fig. 8).

for Making Card:

1. Fold paper for card in half. Card shown has a top fold.
2. Glue three pinwheels across front of card.
3. Draw a border around front of card 1/4" in from edges with a fine point permanent ink pen.
4. Cut out 1/4" squares of paper and glue one to center of each pinwheel. Cut four triangles of paper and glue one in each corner inside border. ❏

Fig. 1

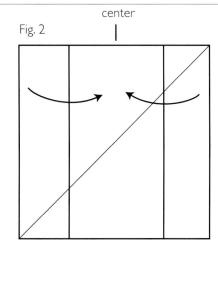

Fig. 2

center

Fig. 3

center

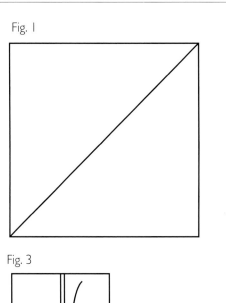

Fig. 4

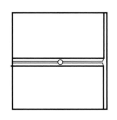

Fig. 5

center

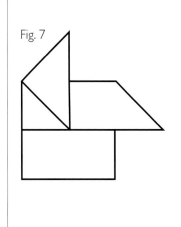

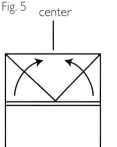

Fig. 6

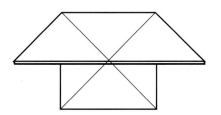

Fig. 7

Fig. 8

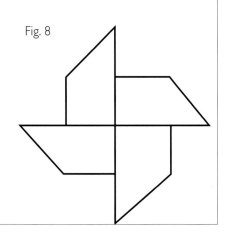

Heart Card

Designed by Susan S. Mickey

SUPPLIES

Square of paper, 8"

INSTRUCTIONS

1. Cut out according to pattern. Mark fold lines.
2. Score on dotted lines before folding (be sure not to cut all the way through). For lines that will fold to outside, score on inside. For lines that will fold to inside, score on outside.
3. Fold as marked. Folds A & B will touch each other when folded correctly. ❑

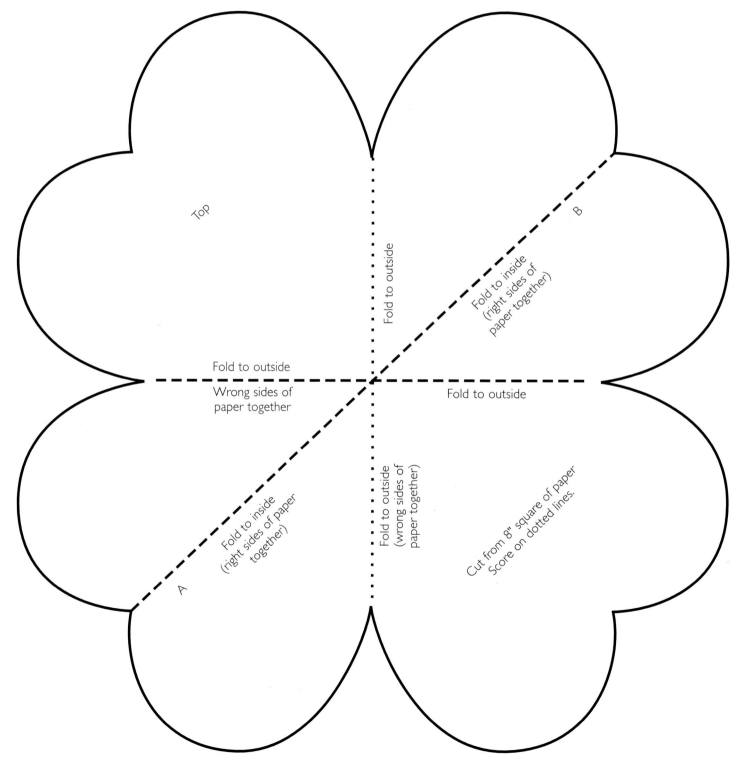

Envelope Patterns
Designed by Lisa Koo

Before you start folding, you can decorate the paper with stenciling, stamping, or freehand drawing, if desired.

INSTRUCTIONS

for Square, Pentagon, & Hexagon (Figs. 1, 2 & 3, respectively):

1. Make pattern of desired shape.
2. Place pattern wrong side up on posterboard (your choice of color), and trace the shape. Cut out.
3. Fold, following the lines on diagrams. Crease the lines well. Unfold.
4. Refold, working around the shape and overlapping the half circles; tuck the last one under the first one.

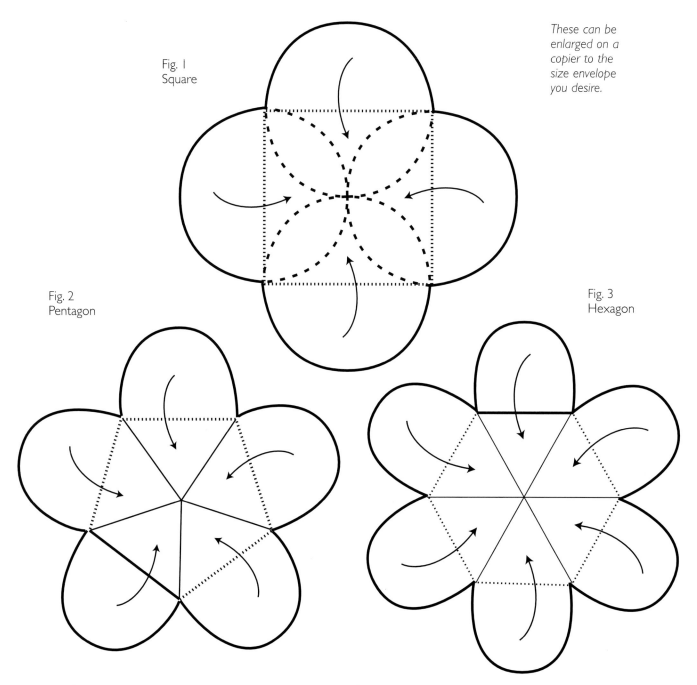

Fig. 1
Square

These can be enlarged on a copier to the size envelope you desire.

Fig. 2
Pentagon

Fig. 3
Hexagon

Fig. 4
Rectangular

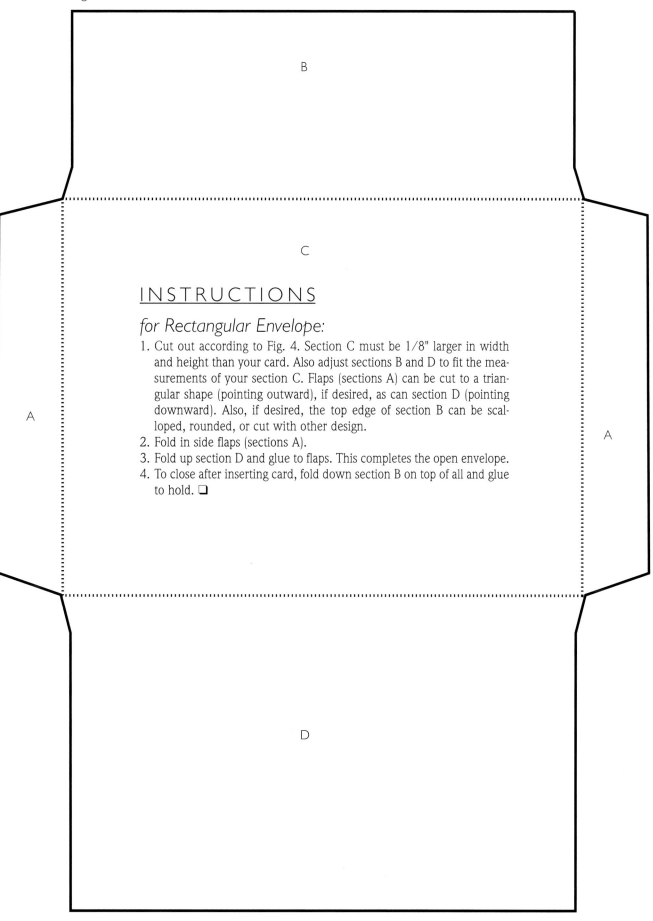

B

C

INSTRUCTIONS

for Rectangular Envelope:

1. Cut out according to Fig. 4. Section C must be 1/8" larger in width and height than your card. Also adjust sections B and D to fit the measurements of your section C. Flaps (sections A) can be cut to a triangular shape (pointing outward), if desired, as can section D (pointing downward). Also, if desired, the top edge of section B can be scalloped, rounded, or cut with other design.
2. Fold in side flaps (sections A).
3. Fold up section D and glue to flaps. This completes the open envelope.
4. To close after inserting card, fold down section B on top of all and glue to hold. ❑

A

A

D

GIFTWRAPS
&
TOPPERS

Whether decorating a gift package or a mason jar that is filled with your homemade peach preserves, you'll find wonderful toppers for them among these projects.

Tea Bag Folded star toppers can be used on gift boxes or giftbags. There is a package medallion to fold. And jars were never so pretty as with a folded star topper or a doily for you to create from folded paper.

It's one of life's extra touches that makes all the difference. And fun, too!

Tea Bag Folded Package Toppers

Designed by Lani Temple

SUPPLIES

Eight squares of decorative paper, 3",
  2-1/2" or 2", depending on the size
  topper you are making
White craft glue
Hot glue and glue gun
Gift bags and boxes
Ribbon

INSTRUCTIONS

1. Cut eight squares of paper. See Fig. 1.

2. Fold a square in half diagonally; unfold.
   See Fig. 2

3. Fold each side point to center, meeting
   at crease formed in step 2. See Fig. 3.

4. Fold the right edge down so the top
   point touches the left side point; unfold.
   See Fig. 4.

5. Repeat fold with the left edge; unfold.
   See Fig. 5

6. Fold the left edge down again, pulling
   left center point out and creasing it
   down. See Fig. 6.

7. Squash the top right point to the left,
   pulling its top layer forward and creasing it down in line with the center
   (reverse-folding in the right side). See
   Fig. 7.

8. Make eight pieces, following steps 1-7.
   Interlock each piece: Turn the piece so
   that the long end points upward. Slip
   the lower left edge inside the right diamond of adjacent piece, aligning bottom points. The right diamond overlaps
   the left one. Repeat with all pieces. Dot
   glue in folds to secure. See Fig. 8.

9. Hot glue to bag or package. ❑

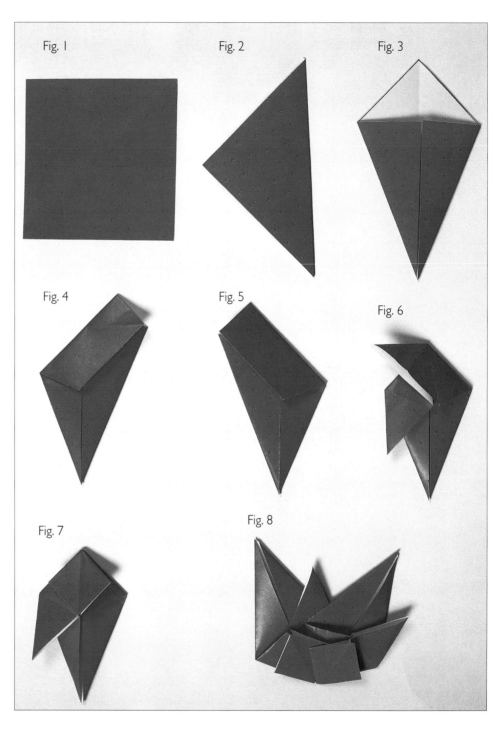

Fig. 1 Fig. 2 Fig. 3 Fig. 4 Fig. 5 Fig. 6 Fig. 7 Fig. 8

A Package Medallion

Designed by Patty Cox

SUPPLIES

Eight squares two-sided paper, different color on each side, 2" each

Wooden bead, 3/8" (stained one of the paper colors)

Hemp cord (the other paper color than that of the bead)

Handmade paper to wrap package (color of the bead)

Optional: Dye (the other paper color than that of the handmade paper)

White craft glue

Clear acrylic spray sealer

INSTRUCTIONS

1. Fold paper in half both ways (Fig. 1). Crease and unfold.
2. Fold paper in half diagonally both ways (Fig. 2). Crease and unfold.
3. Fold in half again bottom edge to top edge (Fig. 3).
4. Push corners into center, forming a triangle (Fig. 4).
5. Lift one corner and open fold (Fig. 5). Press fold flat in center. Turn the piece over and repeat on other side.
6. Fold top point down on each side (Fig. 6).
7. Make eight folded pieces and interlock and glue together (Fig. 7). Glue bead to center of medallion.
8. Wrap package with handmade paper that matches one color of the medallion. Optional: Spatter package with dye of the other medallion paper color.
9. Tie cord around package and glue medallion on top. ❑

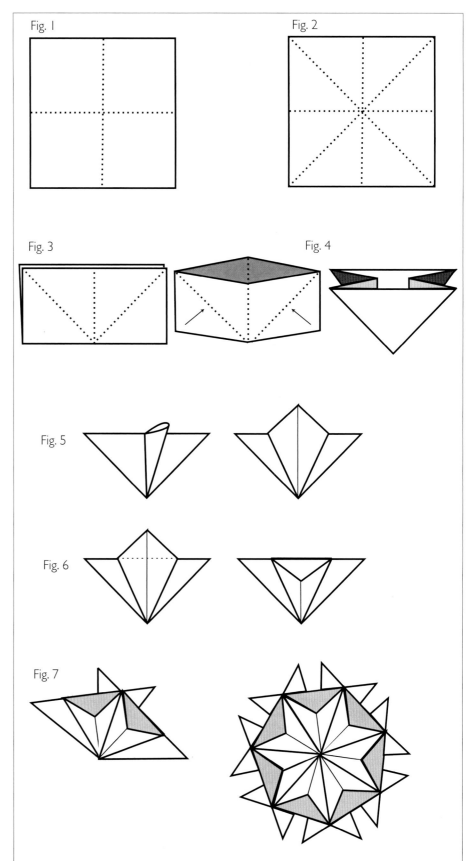

Fig. 1

Fig. 2

Fig. 3

Fig. 4

Fig. 5

Fig. 6

Fig. 7

Peachy Jar Toppers

Designed by Patty Cox

SUPPLIES

Eight 2" squares of thin paper
Craft bond glue stick
Watercolors: yellow and fuchsia
Paint brush
Clear acrylic spray sealer
Bright gold fabric circle, 6" diam.
Pinking shears
Small amount batting
Mason jar of canned goods

PREPARATION

1. Fold each of the 2" squares in half diagonally, then fold in half again. You will have a triangle.
2. Paint each triangle with yellow watercolor. While wet, dip top point of triangle into fuchsia watercolor paint, allowing paint to bleed into the yellow. Unfold and let dry.

INSTRUCTIONS

for Making Topper:

1. Fold in half, top to bottom. Crease and unfold. Fold in half, side to side. Crease and unfold. (Fig. 1)
2. Fold diagonally. Crease and unfold. Fold diagonally in the opposite direction. Crease and unfold. (Fig. 2)
3. Fold in half with bottom edge to top edge (Fig. 3).
4. Push bottom corners to inside center top (Fig. 4a), creating the shape shown (Fig. 4b).
5. Interlock and glue two triangles together, using a glue stick (Fig. 5).
6. Continue to add interlocked triangles, creating the circle shown. Press flat in a book and allow to dry. When dry, open each triangle. Spray the medallion with clear acrylic spray sealer.

for Finishing Jar:

1. Cut a 6" circle from bright gold fabric, using pinking shears. Place a small wad of batting on sealed jar lid. Place fabric over top. Screw jar rim over lid and fabric.
2. Glue medallion on center top of puffed lid. ❑

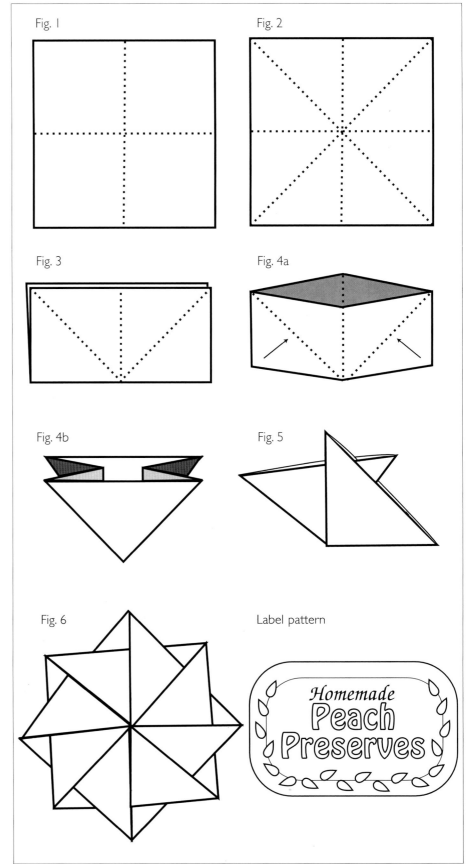

Fig. I

Fig. 2

Fig. 3

Fig. 4a

Fig. 4b

Fig. 5

Fig. 6

Label pattern

Homemade **Peach Preserves**

Doily Jar Cover

Designed by Patty Cox

See photo on page 49

SUPPLIES

Square of tissue paper, 8"
Ribbon, 1/8" or 1/4" wide, enough to tie around jar top in a
   bow
Decorative punch
Scissors

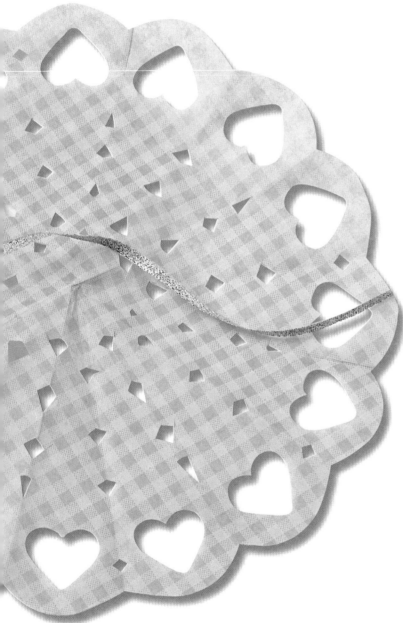

Photo 1

Photo 2

50

INSTRUCTIONS

1. Cut an 8" square of paper.
2. Fold square in half. Photo 1.
3. Continue folding in half until you have folded the square into 1/16ths. Photo 2.
4. Use a circle or oval template or a French curve to draw an even curve at the end of the folded piece (opposite the point). Cut along drawn line. This will create the scallops around the outside of doily. Photo 3.
5. Use a decorative punch to punch a design into scalloped end. Photo 4.
6. Use scissors to cut little designs into the folds on both sides of piece. Photo 5.
7. Open out the piece. Place on jar and tie it in place with ribbon, tying ribbon ends into a bow. Photo 6. ❏

Photo 3

Photo 5

Photo 4

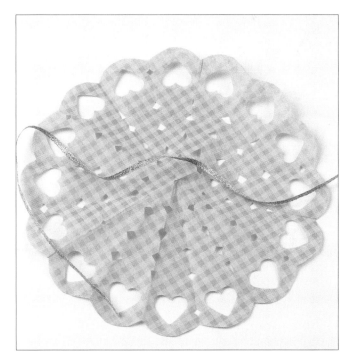

Photo 6: Finished Doily

PAPER GARDEN

The season doesn't have to be right for you to have special flowers. You can make and enjoy these beautiful folded flowers any time of year.

Find folded roses, used here to decorate a shadowbox display, as well as a bouquet of tissue paper roses and another bouquet of handmade-paper lilies. Make whimsy flowers in a pot with Tea Bag Folded star-petaled flowers. Folded lotus flowers grace a framed favorite saying. Folded paper grapes and morning glories make gift cards beautiful.

Flowers are always a joy, and these are even more special because you made them yourself.

Large Folded Rose

MEMENTO SHADOW BOX

Designed by Patty Cox

SUPPLIES

Red handmade paper for roses (paper should be pliable)

Green handmade paper for leaves (paper should be pliable)

White craft glue

Straight pins

Styrofoam® brand plastic foam ball, 2" (cut in half)

Grapevine twigs and tendrils

Shadow box with selected display items

Instructions on page 56

oh, my love is like a red, red rose,
that's newly sprung in June:
oh, my love is like a melody
that's sweetly played in tune.

as fair art thou, my bonnie lass,
so deep in love am I;
and I will love thee still, my dear,
'til all the seas gang dry.

'til all the seas gang dry, my dear,
and the rocks melt with the sun;
and I will love thee still, my dear,
while the sands of life shall run.

and fare thee well, my only love
and fare thee well a while.
and I will come again, my love,
tho' it were ten thousand mile.

Robert Burns

Large Folded Rose

Supplies listed on page 54

PREPARATION AND CENTER:

1. Cut a 2" foam ball in half. Cover the domed side of ball with a 5" square of red paper. Tape ends on back. This is temporary and will be removed later.
2. Rose Center: Cut a 1-1/2" square of red paper. Fold in half diagonally, forming a triangle. With straight edge of triangle at top, begin at one side point and roll triangle into a tube. Glue bottom of tube to center of covered half-ball. Secure with a straight pin.

INSTRUCTIONS

for Rose Petals:

1. Cut 1-1/2" squares of red paper (15 to 30 depending on size of rose you are making).
2. For each petal, fold square in half diagonally (Fig. 1).
3. Fold corners to center (Fig. 2).
4. Fold bottom point to back. Glue folded bottom onto paper-covered base. Secure with straight pin. (Fig. 3)
5. Glue and pin petals around rose center, overlapping petals and *curving* them around the center. (Fig. 4).
6. Make and add as many petals as needed to make the size rose desired. Let glue dry, then remove all straight pins.
7. Remove paper square with rose, from foam dome. Trim square into a circle about the size of the rose. Tuck edges under rose and glue.

for Rosebuds:

No foam base is needed for a rosebud. Make the center as directed for the rose. Make several petals as for the rose and glue them, overlapping each other, around the rose center.

for Leaves:

1. Cut a 1-1/2" square of green paper for each leaf. Fold in half diagonally. With straight edge of triangle at top, fold upper corners to center-bottom point. (Fig. 6)
2. Fold side points to back (Fig. 7).
3. Fold lower point to back (Fig. 8).

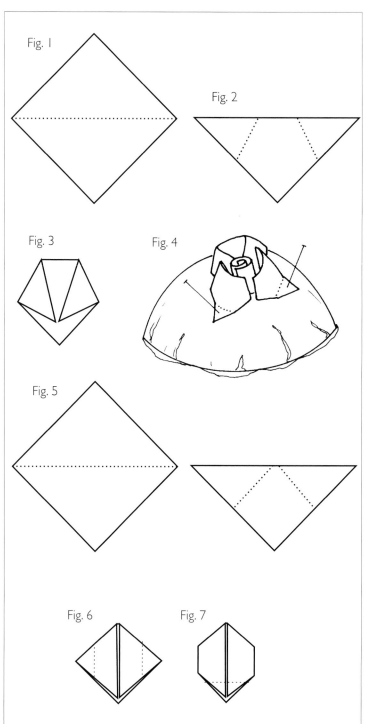

FINISHING SHADOWBOX

1. Arrange chosen display items in shadowbox.
2. Glue roses and leaves on and around grapevine twigs placed to accent items in shadowbox. ❏

Mini Folded Rose

NAPKIN RINGS & GIFT CARD

Designed by Patty Cox

SUPPLIES

For Rose:
Rose colored handmade paper,
 1/4" x 16" strip per rose
White craft glue

For Napkin Ring:
Ivory green handmade paper,
 1/2" x 28" strip per napkin ring
White craft glue

For Gift Card:
Ivory green handmade paper,
 6-3/4" x 4" piece with torn edges
Vellum, 5-3/4" x 3-3/4"
Scrap strips of gold paper to trim
 window of card
Black calligraphy pen for message

INSTRUCTIONS

for Mini Rose:

1. Fold a 2" end of paper strip at a 90-degree angle to other end (Fig. 1).
   The 2" end is a tail to hold. You will work with the other end of paper.

2. Roll and glue paper into a small tube around upper end of tail for rose center (Fig. 2).

3. Begin making petals by gently turning paper strip back at a 45-degree angle and wrapping around center (Fig. 3). *Wet-Fold Option: A glue-and-water mixture makes the paper strip pliable and adheres paper together as the rose is formed. After making the tail and rose center, apply one part glue + one part water on remaining paper strip with a paint brush or fingers. Make rose as directed. When finished, place on wax paper until dry.*

4. Continue rolling strip around center and turning strip back at a 45-degree angle to create another petal point (Fig. 4). When rose is desired size, glue end of paper strip to beginning tail. Clip paper ends. Glue rose to item being decorated. Add silk or paper leaves, if desired. ❏

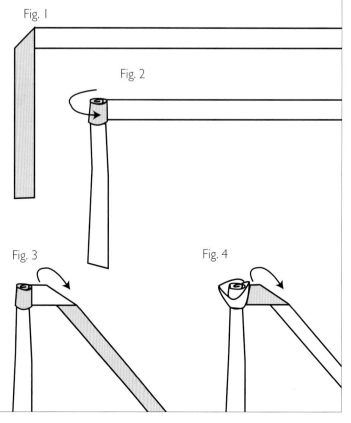

Fig. 1

Fig. 2

Fig. 3

Fig. 4

Heart-Petal Rose

Designed by Ellen Ishino Rankart

SUPPLIES

Tissue paper, color desired

Green Stem wire for each rose (such as paper wrapped wire)

Thick white glue

Florist wire, thin

Floral tape, green

INSTRUCTIONS

1. Trace patterns on tracing paper and cut out.

2. Fold 4" wide strips of tissue paper in half lengthwise. Trace petal patterns onto tissue paper, placing straight edge on fold of paper. Cut out petals. See Photo 1.

3. Open out heart-shaped petals.

4. Twist bottoms of small petals around stem wire, overlapping them. Add dots of glue to hold if necessary. Continue adding petals until you have used all of them. See Photo 2.

Continued on next page

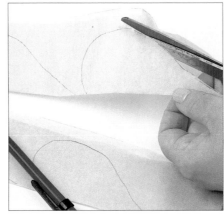

Photo 1: Cut petals from tissue paper.

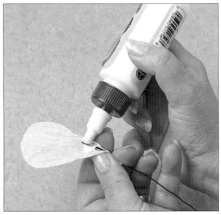

Photo 2: Wrap small petals around the stem wire. Secure with dots of glue.

Photo 3: Add medium petals around center, twisting bottom point of tissue paper around wire.

Photo 4: Add larger petals, overlapping around other petals.

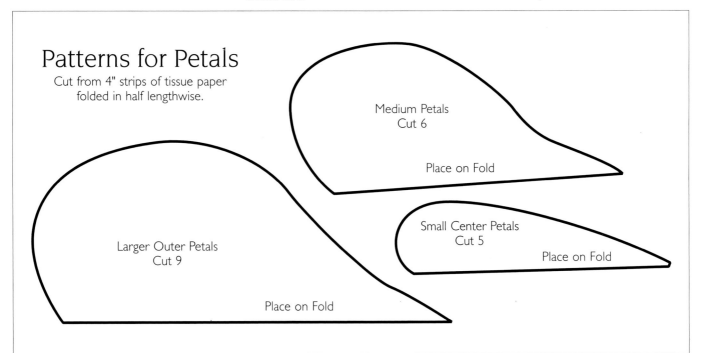

Patterns for Petals

Cut from 4" strips of tissue paper folded in half lengthwise.

Medium Petals
Cut 6

Place on Fold

Larger Outer Petals
Cut 9

Small Center Petals
Cut 5

Place on Fold

Place on Fold

5. Next add the medium size petals around the small petals. Twist bottom points of petals around the wire. Wrap each petal around the previous, overlapping petals. See Photo 3.

6. Add the large petals in the same manner, twisting bottom of petals around stem wire. See Photo 4.

7. Secure petals onto stem wire by wrapping with wire. Wrap stem with floral tape. See Photo 5.

8. Curl the largest petals around a dowel or thin straw at the outer edges of petals to simulate full bloom. See Photo 6. ❏

Photo 5: Secure petals by wrapping base of petals with thin florists wire.

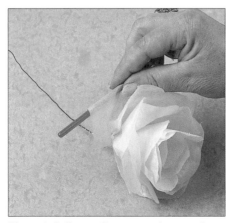

Photo 6: Roll top of outer petals around dowel to curl edges.

Photo 7: Finished rose.

Paper Lily

Designed by Ellen Ishino Rankart

SUPPLIES

Square of paper per lily (7" square is easiest to work with, but any size is fine)
Floral stem wire
Floral tape

INSTRUCTIONS

1. Start with a square of paper. See Fig. 1.
2. Fold paper into a triangle. See Fig. 2.
3. Fold paper again into a smaller triangle. See Fig. 3.
4. With the paper oriented as shown in Fig. 3, push the right, top point to the center. It will create a fold that looks like Fig. 4.
5. Turn paper over and repeat this same technique with the other point of the triangle. It will result in a piece that looks like Fig. 5.
6. Fold the right side of top piece to center to create a fold that looks like Fig. 6.
7. Unfold the flap that you created in step 6—it was a pre-fold to make this step easier. Now push the right point of the crease to the top center to create a fold that looks like Fig. 7. The right side crease is now the crease that is at the center on the outside.
8. Complete all four sides like step 7. You will have to unfold the previous folds as you complete each side. Folds will easily fall back into place. Be sure sides are even. You will have a piece that looks like Fig. 8.
9. Pre-fold bottom right corners in to the center. This pre-folding helps crease the paper to make the next step easier. See Fig. 9.
10. Open folds make in step 9. Push up at the center to create a small kite-shaped fold.
11. Complete all four sides of piece. Then fold the top of kite down. See Fig. 11.
12. Turn the piece so the "legs" are on top and the solid point is at bottom. You will work with the piece in this position. The solid point will be the base of the flower. Now bring the right point to the left side. This will create a flat front. See Fig. 12.
13. Bring the top flap down. Repeat this on the backside. See Fig. 13.

14. You have a little kite shape again. Open out the bottom fold so you have more paper exposed inside the bottom of this kite shape. See Fig. 14.
15. Do this same technique on four sides. See Fig. 15.
16. The points that were exposed, fold them up, so point is at top. These will be the petals. See Fig. 16.
17. On each petal, fold side creases in to center. See Fig. 17.
18. Open out petals, bending, rolling and forming petals into a flower shape. See Fig. 18.
❏

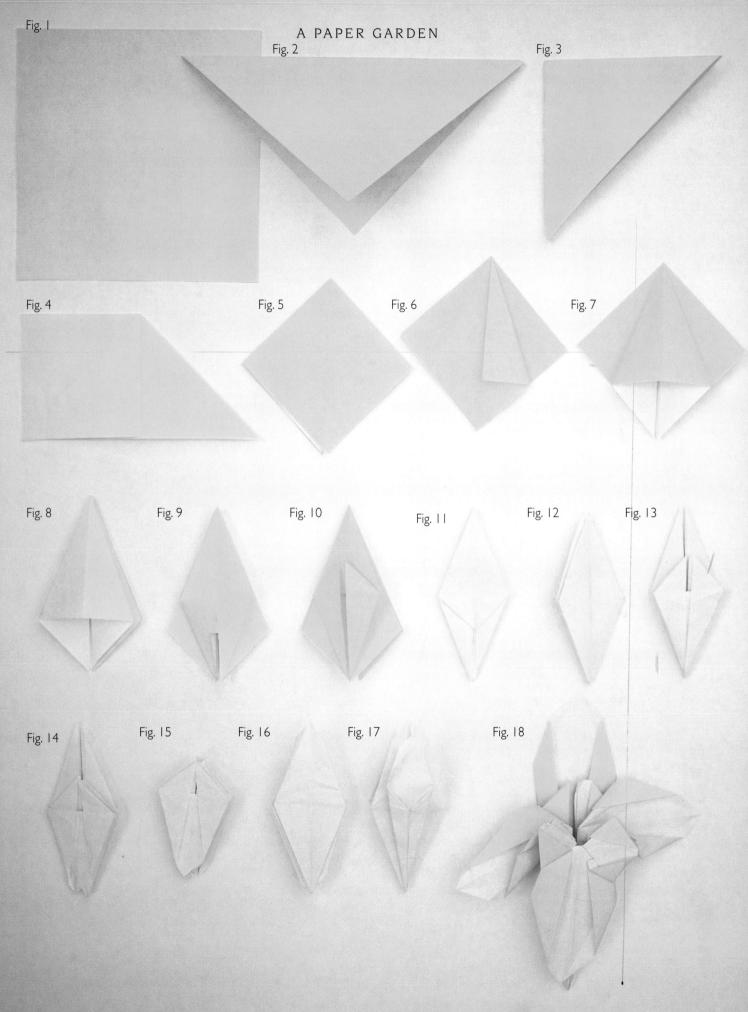

Fig. 1 Fig. 2 Fig. 3 Fig. 4 Fig. 5 Fig. 6 Fig. 7 Fig. 8 Fig. 9 Fig. 10 Fig. 11 Fig. 12 Fig. 13 Fig. 14 Fig. 15 Fig. 16 Fig. 17 Fig. 18

Whimsy Flowers in a Pot
Designed by Lani Temple

SUPPLIES

Solid red, yellow, and orange papers, eight 2-1/2" squares per flower
Flower print paper in red, yellow and orange, eight 3" squares per flower
Paper punches: circle and flower designs
Twelve green satin rose leaves
Six 18-gauge floral wires, 18" long
Green grosgrain ribbon
Floral foam
Thick white glue
Double stick tape
Mounting adhesive
Wood flower pot
Spanish moss
Wire cutters

INSTRUCTIONS

for Making Folded Flower:

1. Cut eight 2-1/2" of solid paper or eight 3" squares of print paper. See Fig. 1.
2. Fold square in half, right to left. See Fig. 2
3. Fold top left corner down to center fold. Unfold. See Fig. 3.
4. Fold same corner down to fold line made in last step. See Fig. 4.
5. Fold down again to fold made in step 3. (Fold made in step 4 is now underneath.) See Fig. 5.
6. Flip piece so that folded corner is at bottom and underneath, keeping fold at right. Repeat steps 3, 4, and 5 on top corner. The top corner and the bottom underneath corner will be folded just alike. See Fig. 6.
7. After making eight of these, interlock them as follows: Slide an unfolded corner under folded corner. Make sure to slide unfolded corners inside folded corners on both sides to get a two-sided pattern. Dot glue in folds to secure. See Fig. 7.

for Assembling Flowers & Pot:

1. Make a flower of each solid color and one of each print color; make an extra one of one print paper (7 total).
2. Cut floral foam to fit snugly in flower pot.
3. Wrap two wired rose leaves around center of each floral stem. Trim stems

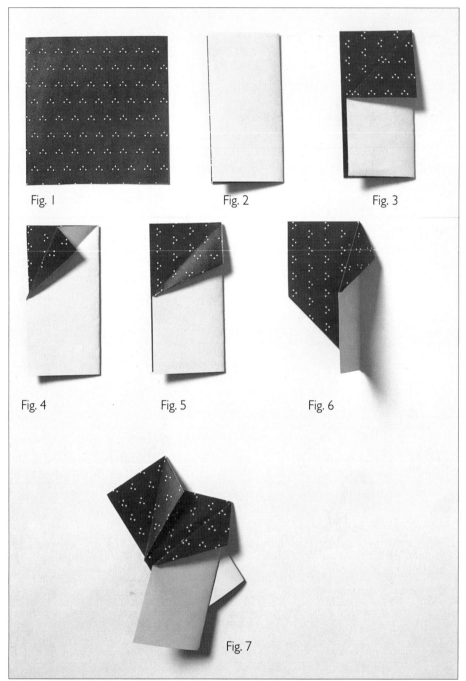

Fig. 1   Fig. 2   Fig. 3

Fig. 4   Fig. 5   Fig. 6

Fig. 7

to different lengths with wire cutters. To cover wire, wrap ribbon tightly around wire and secure with glue or tape. Make six stems with leaves. Push stems into floral foam.

4. Fold a 1" piece of two sided tape around top of each floral stem and attach flowers with floral stem between flower layers.
5. To make center of flower, stick small pieces of colored paper to one side of mounting adhesive. Punch circles and flowers. Pull off back of mounting adhesive and stick a contrasting color circle to center of each punched flowers. Stick a punched flower/circle to center of each folded flower.
6. Glue the extra folded flower to front of pot. Edge pot by gluing green ribbon around top of pot. Add Spanish moss around flower stems to cover floral foam. ❏

Lotus Flower

FRAMED SAYING

Designed by Patty Cox

SUPPLIES

Watercolor paper, 1-1/2" square per
  flower (10 used on framed saying)
Watercolor paints: Yellow and fuchsia
Paint brush
White craft glue
18 pale yellow seed beads
Two 18" lengths green florist's wire
Three pale yellow heart buttons (with
  shanks cut off)
Framed 5" x 7" saying (or print your own
  on vellum and place over a 5" x 7"
  piece of handmade paper)

INSTRUCTIONS

1. Fold paper in half, top to bottom with
   right sides together. Crease and
   unfold. Fold paper in half, side to side
   with right sides together. Crease and
   unfold. (Fig. 1a). Fold paper diagonally, wrong sides together. Crease and
   unfold. Fold paper diagonally in the
   other direction, wrong sides together.
   Crease and unfold. (Fig. 1b).

2. Paint each paper square with a golden
   yellow wash. While paint is wet, paint
   fuchsia on each crease, allowing paint
   to bleed into the yellow wash. Let dry.

3. Fold again on one of the diagonal folds
   with point at top (Fig. 2).

4. Open one corner and push it inward
   (Fig. 3). It will be perpendicular to
   main plane. Turn to front and press it
   flat (Fig. 4).

5. Repeat with other corner (Fig. 5).

6. Make ten flowers, then make three of
   them smaller by folding the sides of
   outer petals to the back.

7. Spiral-wrap florist's wire around a pencil; slide off pencil. Cut one wire in
   half. Open the spiral in the center of
   each length. Arrange on framed saying, and glue in place.

8. Glue lotus flowers onto paper and
   frame around the wire stems (refer to
   photo of project).

9. Glue three seed beads above each
   flower.

10. Glue the heart buttons around flowers
    (refer to photo of project). ❑

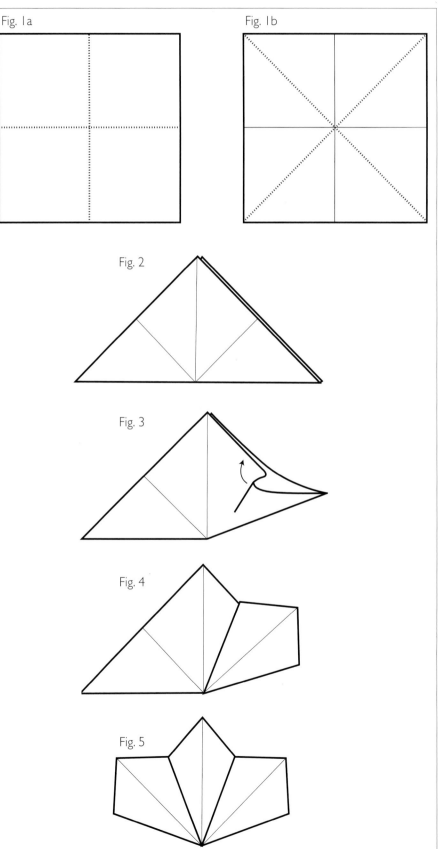

Fig. 1a

Fig. 1b

Fig. 2

Fig. 3

Fig. 4

Fig. 5

we laugh
we cry
we make
time fly
best friends
are we
my sister
and me

Grapes on a Gift Card
Designed by Patty Cox

SUPPLIES

Nine strips purple paper, each 1/8" x 8"
Three 3/4" squares green paper
White craft glue
Green florist's wire, 6" length
Nine purple seed beads
Toothpick
Handmade paper with torn edges, 4"x 6-1/2"
Vellum, 3-1/2" square

INSTRUCTIONS

for Making Grape (Fold-Over Chain):

1. Fold paper length in half at a 90-degree angle (Fig. 1).
2. Fold side A over B (Fig. 2).
3. Fold side B over A (Fig. 3).
4. Fold side A over B. Continue folding chain in this manner to ends of paper (Fig. 4).
5. Glue ends of each chain together to form the grape (Fig. 5).

for Making Grape Leaf:

1. Fold 3/4" square in half, forming a triangle (Fig. 6).
2. Accordion-fold leaf from center bottom (Fig. 7).
3. Finished leaf is shown in Fig. 8.

for Making Gift Card:

1. Make nine fold-over chain grapes with the nine strips of purple paper.
2. Glue a purple seed bead in the center of each.
3. Fold three grape leaves.
4. Spiral-wrap a 6" length of green florist's wire around a toothpick. Slide off toothpick for a tendril.
5. Fold the 4" x 6-1/2" handmade paper in half to 3-1/4" x 4" (left side fold). Cut a 2" x 2-1/2" window in center of front.
6. Fold a 3/8" edge upward on the 3-1/2" x 3-1/2" vellum. Glue fold inside front of card so that vellum is positioned behind window.
7. Glue grapes, leaves, and tendril on vellum as shown in photo of project.
8. Trim inside edges of window with torn pieces of purple paper.

Grapes are also shown in burgundy on a wine tasting invitation with painted leaves and tendril. ❏

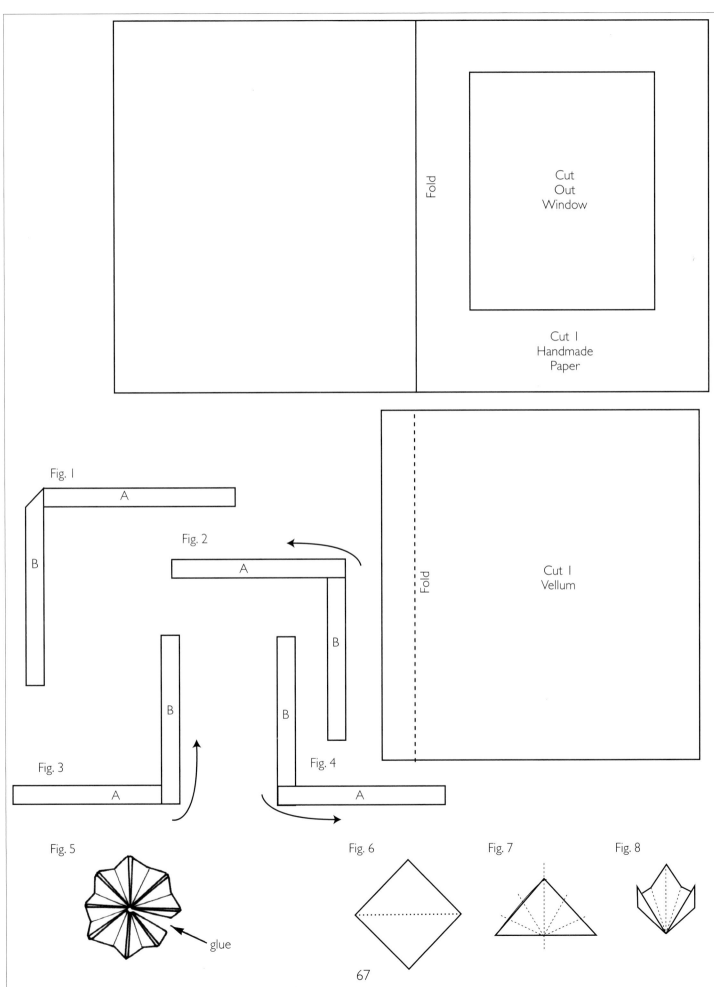

Fold

Cut
Out
Window

Cut 1
Handmade
Paper

Fig. 1

A

B

Fig. 2

A

B

Fold

Cut 1
Vellum

B

B

Fig. 3

A

Fig. 4

A

Fig. 5

glue

Fig. 6

Fig. 7

Fig. 8

Morning Glories

Designed by Lisa Koo

SUPPLIES

Tissue paper (preferably lavender, blue, or pink), enough for three 3" squares

Scrap of light green paper, enough for three 1/2" squares

Card or framed handmade paper to decorate with morning glories (shown is a corrugated frame with handmade paper behind the opening)

Ruler

Thick white glue

Light green permanent pen (or light green paint and an artist's liner brush)

INSTRUCTIONS

for one Morning Glory;
(make 3):

NOTE: If you have difficulty handling the tissue paper because it is too thin, you can double the paper.)

1. Fold the paper diagonally (right sides together, if there is a right and wrong side). Crease. Fold the bottom corner to the top corner (Fig. 1). Crease.

2. Open the top flap and flatten it to make a square. Crease well (Fig. 2).

3. Turn over the paper and repeat step 2 on the reverse side (Fig. 3).

4. Fold the left edge to the center and crease (Fig. 4).

5. Turn paper over with open edges at top and two points on inside at top and fold the new left edge to center as on other side. It will look like Fig. 5.

6. Hold the bottom point tightly (indicated by dotted line in Fig. 6). Pull the points at top inside to the bottom, flattening both sides to form the petals.

7. Fold the corners at tips of petals to the back of flower (Fig. 7) to complete the petals.

8. For leaves, cut a 1/2" square of green paper per leaf (make 3 leaves).

9. Pinch one corner of the square (Fig. 8) and glue to hold (Fig. 9).

10. Glue flowers and leaves on card, frame, or other object. Draw stems and tendrils on background with a light green pen (or paint with light green paint and a liner brush). ❑

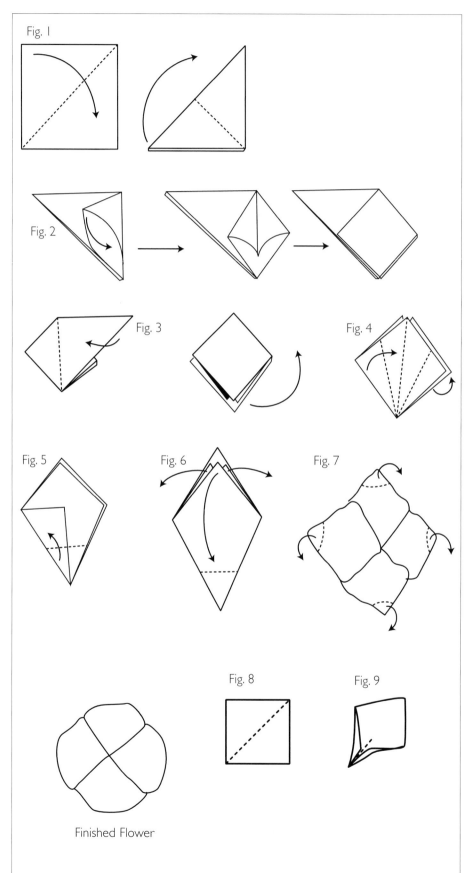

Fig. 1

Fig. 2

Fig. 3

Fig. 4

Fig. 5

Fig. 6

Fig. 7

Fig. 8

Fig. 9

Finished Flower

Lampshades
&
Luminaries

Light joins artistic design for especially beautiful projects with these lampshades, luminaries, and candle embellishments.

Shades of a Japanese garden, literally – that describes the folded and dyed paper shade you'll find in this section. There is also a more traditional western-world style accordion-pleated lampshade. Because it's made of paper, by you, the colors and/or patterns can be perfectly coordinated with the decor in the room where it will be used.

For the luminaries, you may either use translucent paper or cut lovely designs in opaque paper to let the candlelight shine through. These are beautiful at night. They can line your walk or decorate a window on a holiday occasion, or add a special atmosphere to a patio party.

The candles in glass candle holders are made more beautiful by shining through translucent covers with decorative paper borders, and set on elaborate folded star mats which match the borders.

Isn't it the special touches that make life worthwhile?

Accordion Pleated Shade

By Ellen Ishino Rankart

SUPPLIES

Translucent paper such as parchment paper, vellum, or glassine.
    Choose a paper that holds a crease.
Wire lampshade frame
Hot glue an glue gun
Ruler

INSTRUCTIONS

1. Measure the largest circumference and height of existing shade.
2. Cut a paper strip twice the circumference and 1/2" taller than the measured height.
3. Accordion-pleat the paper strip (alternating inward and outward folds). Your folds should be in proportion to the size of the shade. A small shade would have 1/4" folds, a medium shade would have 1/2" folds, and a larger shade would have 3/4" folds.
4. Divide the number of pleats and the frame into four equal sections. Hot glue pleats to these sections first so that the pleats will be distributed equally around frame. Hot glue both top and bottom of paper shade around wire lampshade. ❑

Folded & Dyed Lampshade

By Ellen Ishino Rankart

*Here paper is folded and dyed in a tie-dye technique. The dyed paper is then used to create a hanging lampshade. This tie-dye technique was created by Marie Browning from her book, **Hand Decorating Paper**, published by Sterling Publishing Company.*

SUPPLIES

Paper that is thin, translucent, and absorbent without any added sizes or coatings (Japanese rice paper or mulberry papers are good, as is the paper used to cover examination tables at doctors' offices)

Good quality drawing inks (diluted with water in a 50/0 mix, or full strength for more vibrant colored paper)

Freezer paper (to cover work area and to lay out paper to dry)

Plastic gloves (to protect hands from dye)

Small bowl of clean water

Plastic containers (disposable cups or recycled plastic containers work well)

Wooden clothespins

Plastic sandwich bags

Two metal lampshade hoops, identical in size (One should be for the top, and one for the bottom. The top ring should look like Fig. 1. If you cannot find a lampshade hoop, use a plain hoop and use wire to attach the light bulb fixture to frame)

Heavy wire

Light bulb fixture and attached cord

Low wattage bulb

Hot glue sticks and glue gun

Thick white glue

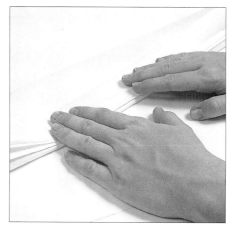

Photo 1: Accordion pleat paper.

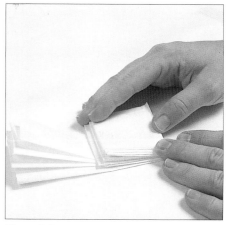

Photo 2: Fold paper in other direction to form a square.

Photo 3: Dip paper into clear water.

Photo 4: Dip corners and folds of paper into ink to dye it.

INSTRUCTIONS

for Dying Paper:

1. Determine size of shade. the size of your hoops will determine the circumference of the shade. You will need to determine the height of the lampshade you desire. Cut paper to desired length and a width determined by circumference of hoop plus 1/4" for overlapping. If you paper is extremely wide and hard to handle, you may need to cut it in half to make it easier to handle and to dye.

2. Fold the paper in even accordion pleats along the length of the paper. The pleats should be about 2" wide for a large shade and no smaller than 1" for a small shade. See Photo 1.

3. Then accordion fold again in squares, rectangles, or triangles to create different looks. See Photo 2.

4. Hold the folded paper together with a clothespin.

5. Dip the folded paper into the bowl of clean water and squeeze out excess water. See Photo 3.

Pictured left: A closeup view of folded paper.

6. Starting with the lightest color, dip the corners of the folded paper into the ink. Dip into color quickly so that it will not absorb too much ink. It is best to have the color along the fold and fade to white. See Photo 4.

7. Repeat with other ink colors, working from the lightest to the darkest color.

8. Place the folded paper inside a plastic sandwich bag. Squeeze the folded paper to help the inks spread and to remove excess ink. (You can rinse and reuse the plastic bag for additional tie-dye papers.)

9. Unfold the paper, pleat by pleat. The wet paper can tear easily, so work slowly and carefully. Place the unfolded sheet on freezer paper to dry flat or drape it over a line to dry.

10. When dry, carefully flatten the paper with a hot, DRY iron.

INSTRUCTIONS

for Making Shade:

11. Prepare top hoop of frame if needed, by attaching wire to hold the bulb attachment of light fixture in place. If you have a hoop as shown in Fig. 1, then the electric cord for your light fixture can be threaded through the hole in center. A plug will need to be attached to end of cord.

12. Hot-glue paper to top frame, carefully covering entire frame.

13. Suspend light fixture. Overlap edges of paper where they meet and glue with thick white glue, being sure the overlap is the same amount all the way to bottom of paper.

14. Glue paper to bottom frame. ❏

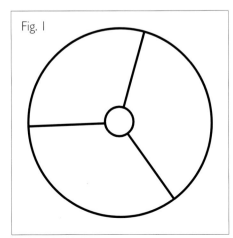

Fig. I

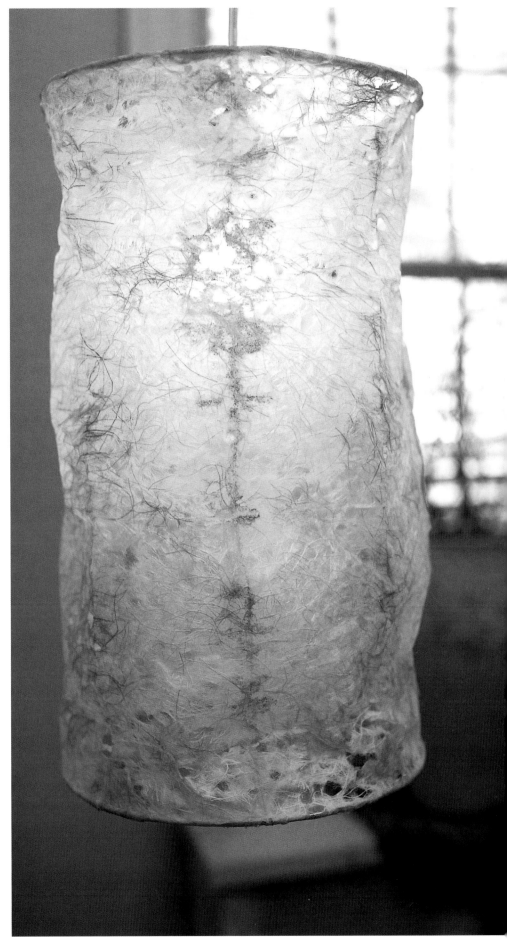

Exotic Luminaries

Designed by Susan S. Mickey

SUPPLIES

Translucent paper such as parchment paper, vellum paper, glassine, thin white paper. Alternative: Use non-translucent paper and cut out designs from your luminary bag for the light to shine through.

Scissors

Ruler

Thick white glue

INSTRUCTIONS

1. Cut a rectangle of paper – 20" x 13-1/2" for a medium size or 23" x 14" for a large bag.

2. Using the diagrams for medium or large giftbag on pages 20 and 21, measure and mark fold lines.

3. If you are going to cut out a design (such as the firefly design – pattern given), trace the pattern on front and/or back section and cut it out before folding bag.

4. Follow the instructions for folding the bag, omitting the handle.

5. Place votive candle inside. ❏

Firefly pattern

Trace on front of luminary and cut out.

Tea Bag Folded Candle Mats & Covers

Designed by Lani Temple

SUPPLIES

Decorative paper squares, 4" (each star mat uses 8 to 16 squares); extra decorative paper for wrapping base of candle holder

Orange vellum (candle holder wrapping)

Glass cylindrical candle holder

Narrow ribbon, color to match papers

White craft glue

Double sided tape

INSTRUCTIONS

for Folded Star Candle Mat:

1. Cut squares. Each mat uses 8 to 16 squares, depending on size of candle holder. Cut squares in half on the diagonal to form triangles. See Fig. 1.

2. Fold each triangle in half; unfold. See Fig. 2.

3. Fold each side point to the top. See Fig. 3.

4. Unfold and turn over. See Fig. 4.

5. On one side of triangle, fold the crease just made to center fold. See Fig. 5.

6. Repeat on other side of triangle with other crease just made. See Fig. 6.

7. Turn over to other side of piece. This will be the front. See Fig. 7.

8. Trace bottom circle of glass candle holder onto a piece of paper to use as a guide. Interlock folded pieces as follows: Slip the unfolded side of one piece under the fold of adjacent piece. Repeat with more pieces, following around the circle pattern you drew, until circle is complete. Dot glue in folds to secure. See Fig. 8.

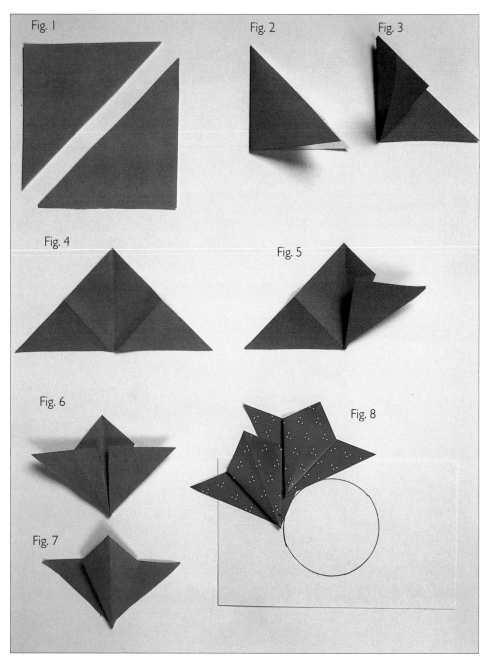

Fig. 1 Fig. 2 Fig. 3 Fig. 4 Fig. 5 Fig. 6 Fig. 7 Fig. 8

INSTRUCTIONS

for Candle Assembly:

1. Measure and cut orange vellum to fit around glass candle holder. Wrap vellum around glass and secure in back with double sided tape.
2. Measure and cut a 1" to 2" band of decorative paper and vellum to fit around glass. Wrap around glass at bottom and secure in back with double sided tape.
3. Cut and glue narrow ribbon around seam between vellum and decorative band.
4. Place candle holder on folded star mat. ❏

Whimsy

Sometimes the best things in life are those which are just for fun. We have some of those projects here – fun to make and just plain fun to have.

You'll enjoy making the pinwheel windmill – so easy a child could make the pinwheels. (In fact, you probably did make some as a child). But these are made of beautiful decorative paper.

The headband is another project full of glee – decorated with folded paper stars and ribbon streamers.

Would you believe that you can fold a square of paper into a swimsuit design? We've done it here, and used it on an invitation to a beach party. It's a fun time all around, from making the invitation to having the party.

Lighten up your life today with these whimsical projects.

Pinwheel Windmill

Designed by Lani Temple

SUPPLIES

Decorative wrapping paper, eight 6" squares per pinwheel, 4 pinwheels needed

Mounting adhesive, four 6" squares per pinwheel, 4 pinwheels needed

Wood embroidery hoop, 12" diam.

Wood dowel, 3/8" diam. – one per pinwheel

Map pins

bugle beads

Gold ribbon

White craft glue or tape

Craft knife and cutting mat

Large needle

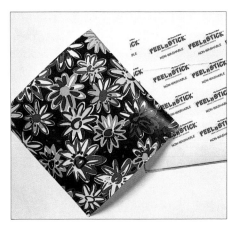

Photo 1: Make double-sided paper by sandwiching mounting adhesive between two squares of paper.

Photo 2: Cut front corner in towards center and fold each corner in to center.

Photo 3: Continue folding in corners

Photo 4: attach all four corners to center to form pinwheel.

INSTRUCTIONS

1. Cover wood hoop and dowel by wrapping ribbon tightly around each. Secure with glue or tape. Glue the hoop to the dowel in two places and secure with wire or tape.
2. To make double-sided paper, peel off one side of mounting adhesive and adhere a square of decorative paper. Turn over and repeat. See Photo 1
3. Find center of square and mark with a needle hole. Using a craft knife, cut diagonally in toward center for 3" from each corner.
4. Working around the square, bend each corner to the center and thread onto a map pin. See Photos 2 & 3.
5. Push the pin through the center of the square. See Photo 4.
6. Add two bugle beads to pin, and pin pinwheel securely to the wood embroidery hoop. The bead will act as a bushing and allow the pinwheel to turn freely.
7. Make three more pinwheels, and pin them all equidistant around the wood hoop. ❑

Folded Star Headband

Designed by Lani Temple

SUPPLIES

Headband (hoop style)

Decorative paper, eight 3" squares per star (approximately 7 stars needed, depending on size of headband)

White craft glue

Hot glue sticks and glue gun

Ribbon for streamers in colors to match paper

INSTRUCTIONS

for Making Star:

Each star requires eight paper squares.

1. Fold the square diagonally both ways. Unfold. See Fig. 1.

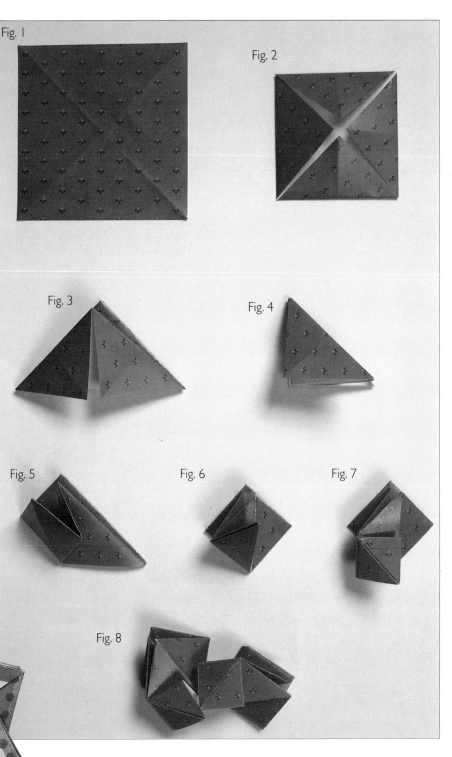

2. Fold all corners to center. See Fig. 2.
3. Fold in half backward along one diagonal, making a triangle. See Fig. 3.
4. Fold triangle in half. See Fig. 4.
5. Square lower corner to upper corner, opening to lie flat. See Fig. 5. Squash upper point down to lower point, opening to lie flat.

Continued on next page

6. Turn over. Fold lower left corner up to center point. See Fig. 6.
7. Squash upper left point down to lower point to lie flat. See Fig. 7.
8. When all eight stars are made, interlock them by slipping extended corner of one piece inside fold of adjacent piece. Repeat with all eight folded pieces. Dot glue in folds to secure. See Fig. 8. ❏

for Assembling Headband:

1. Make folded stars as directed above – approximately seven, depending on size of headband.
2. To cover hoop, wrap ribbon tightly around it and secure with hot glue.
3. Tie long ribbons to back of hoop and knot at ends.
4. Hot-glue finished folded stars around outside of hoop.
5. Tie small bows with extra ribbon and hot-glue them in open spaces between folded stars. ❏

Folded Swimsuit

BEACH PARTY INVITATION

Designed by Patty Cox

SUPPLIES

Square of striped or printed paper, 4"

Spattered tan paper, 7" x 10"

Parchment paper, 4-3/4" x 6-3/4"

Teal paper, dark blue paper, and sandpaper, 4" x 5" piece of each

Two buttons, 1/2" to 3/4" diam.

Shell, approx. 5/8"

Golden embroidery floss

Thick white glue

INSTRUCTIONS

for making Swimsuit:

1. Fold 4" square in half, top to bottom. Crease and unfold. Fold in half, side to side. Crease and unfold. (Fig. 1).

2. Fold the square diagonally. Crease and unfold. Fold it diagonally in the other direction. Crease and unfold. (Fig. 2).

3. Fold in half again, bottom to top (Fig. 3).

4. Push lower corners inward and up to center, forming a triangle (Fig. 4). Turn triangle over so point is at top.

5. Fold sides of top layer triangle to center.

6. Fold points of back layer triangle up to center top (Fig. 6). Turn upside down again.

7. Fold outer points of back layer triangle to center (Fig. 7). Fig. 7 also shows back view.

8. On front, fold top points down (Fig. 8).

9. Open folds of top points (Fig. 9). Press flat and crease. Optional: Bodice cups can be lifted open for added dimension.

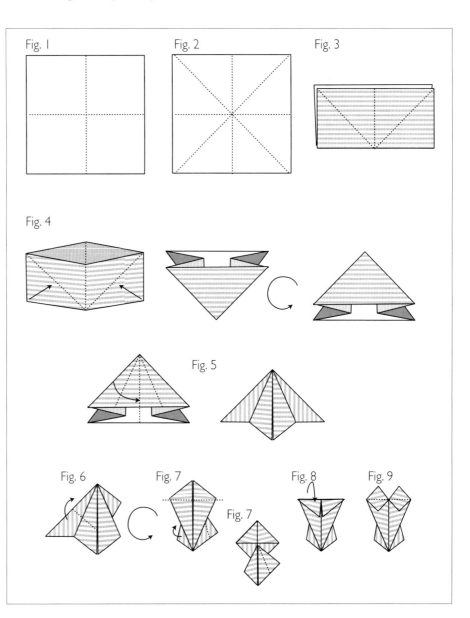

Fig. I Fig. 2 Fig. 3 Fig. 4 Fig. 5 Fig. 6 Fig. 7 Fig. 7 Fig. 8 Fig. 9

for Making Invitation Card:

1. Fold spattered paper in half to measure 5" x 7" with left side fold. Cut a 2-1/4" x 3" window in card front.

2. Frame window with cut "border frames" of teal paper and dark blue paper and with a torn "frame" of sandpaper, gluing these in place on front around window. (Refer to photo of project.)

3. Print "Beach Party" above framed window.

4. Sew buttons on front of card at lower right corner of framed window with embroidery floss. Sew diagonal lines of floss across lower right and upper left corner of frames around window. Glue shell near buttons.

5. Glue parchment paper on inside of card.

6. Glue folded swimsuit on parchment so that it is centered in window when card is closed. ❑

Hanging Mobiles & Light Catchers

Whether adding some extra sunshine to a window in your home or decorating for a special occasion, you'll enjoy making and using these projects.

They are made of folded vellum, a translucent paper that lets light filter through. The light catcher will remind you of sunny days no matter what the weather. And the star mobile has the special charm of a starry night.

Try them and see.

Folded Light Catcher

Designed by Lani Temple

SUPPLIES

Red or orange velum, sixteen 3" squares

Needle and red thread

Assorted red beads

Thick white glue

INSTRUCTIONS

for Making Star:

1. Cut sixteen 3" squares of paper for star. See Fig. 1.
2. Fold square in half diagonally; unfold. See Fig. 2.
3. Fold each side point to the center crease. See Fig. 3.
4. At top, fold each side point to center; unfold. See Fig. 4.
5. At top, fold each side point to the creases created in step 4. Then fold again on original step 4 folds. See Fig. 5.
6. To interlock, place two folded pieces side by side with diagonal edges touching, all flaps on backside. Lay another diamond on top, centered on first two and aligning bottom points of all. Dot glue on thickest folds and hold for 40 seconds. Repeat until you have used all 16 folded pieces. See Fig. 6.

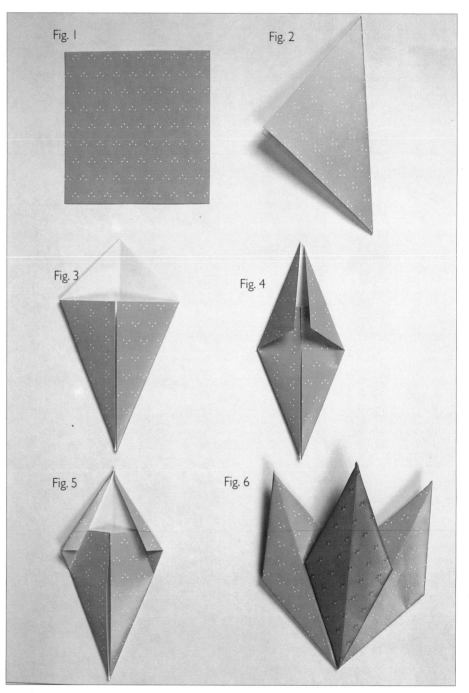

Fig. 1   Fig. 2   Fig. 3   Fig. 4   Fig. 5   Fig. 6

for Assembling Light Catcher:

1. Make star according to directions above.
2. Thread needle and knot end of thread. Thread on several red beads of assorted sizes. Line up top bead with bottom edge of star, then leave space on thread until it reaches center of star. String on one bead and loop thread through bead a second time to secure at that position. Pass needle through center of star. String on another bead and loop thread back through bead to secure. Pass needle back through center of star. Tie a knot a foot above top of star.
3. Hang from knot in center of window.

You may add other stars made in the same manner to the window for interest. ❏

Starlight Mobile

Designed by Lani Temple

SUPPLIES

Blue, silver, and pearl vellum, 3" squares
  (5 squares per star, 5 stars used for
  mobile)

Blue wire, 5" to 10" lengths

Ribbon

Wood dowel, 3/16" diam. x 36" long

Thick white glue

Double sided tape

INSTRUCTIONS

for Making Star:

1. Cut five 3" squares for each star. See
   Fig. 1.

2. Fold square in half diagonally; unfold.
   See Fig. 2.

3. Fold each side point to center; unfold.
   See Fig. 3.

4. Fold each side point in half. Fold again
   on original step-3 fold. See Fig. 4.

5. Turn over so that folds are on backside
   of folded pieces. Place two pieces side
   by side with centers meeting and folds
   just overlapping. Dot glue on thickest folds and hold for 40
   seconds. Repeat with remaining pieces to complete star. See
   Fig. 5.

for Assembling Mobile:

1. Make five folded stars as directed above.

2. To cover dowel, wrap ribbon tightly around it and secure
   with glue or double sided tape.

3. Make a small hole near the top of each star. Gently push wire
   through hole and twist end of wire with needlenose pliers.
   Wrap other end of wire around dowel and twist end for a
   decorative squiggle. Repeat with additional stars and hang
   the mobile in place. ❏

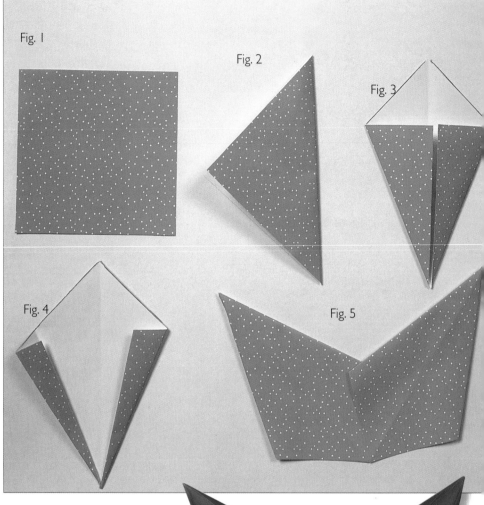

Fig. 1

Fig. 2

Fig. 3

Fig. 4

Fig. 5

*Back of
Finished Star*

PICTURE FRAMES

We all look for special ways to frame and display photos. There are several unique ways in this section.

First, there are decorative gold-paper folded corners for adding elegance to the photos in your albums. (The same folded design can also be used to make beautiful napkin rings.) Then there are folded photo medallions. Tape photos in the center circles of the medallions and glue these frame beauties to a hanging ribbon for a "family photo tree." Two other beautiful photo frame designs are also included.

These make special displays for the images of special people.

Art Deco Photo Corners

Designed by Patty Cox

SUPPLIES

Four squares metallic gold paper, 1-1/2"
White craft glue

INSTRUCTIONS

1. Fold square in half, top to bottom. Crease and unfold. Fold in half, side to side. Crease and unfold. (Fig. 1).
2. Fold the square diagonally. Crease and unfold. Fold it diagonally in the other direction. Crease and unfold. (Fig. 2).
3. Fold in half again, bottom to top (Fig. 3).
4. Push lower corners inward and up to center, forming a triangle (Fig. 4).
5. Lift right top-layer corner and fold to center with point extending above triangle at center-top (Fig. 5). Turn over and repeat with new right top-layer corner.
6. Glue art deco corners on photos, announcements, or invitations placed in albums. ❑

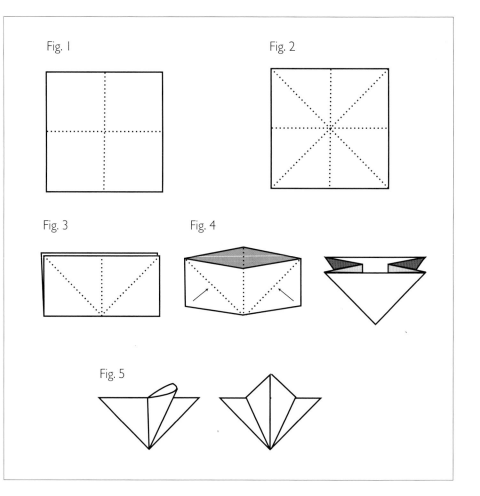

Fig. 1 Fig. 2 Fig. 3 Fig. 4 Fig. 5

Art Deco Napkin Ring

Designed by Patty Cox

Pictured on page 98

SUPPLIES

Gold metallic paper – 3-1/2" square for each ornament; 6-1/2" x 2-1/2" piece for each ring
White craft glue
Low melt glue and glue gun
Paper clips
Angel charm
Clear acrylic spray sealer

INSTRUCTIONS

1. To make the ring, fold long sides of the 6-1/2" strip of paper to center-back. Overlap ends and glue.
2. To make the ornament, follow instructions and Figs. 1-5 of "Art Deco Photo Corners." After the folds in Fig. 5, round the edges of the center V-shaped area and glue the back layer of these pieces to back triangle; hold with paper clips until dry.
3. Accordion-fold diagonal creases on each of the outer sections (Fig. 6). Turn the top points of accordion-folded sections under and glue to secure.
4. Glue folded ornament onto overlapped ends of ring. Glue angel charm to lower edge of folded ornament with low melt glue.
5. Spray napkin ring with clear acrylic sealer. ❑

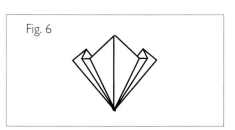

Fig. 6

Art Deco Photo Corners
Used to Trim Cards

Grand Opening

Deco Designs
Stained Glass Showroom

Preston L. Wright
proprietor

1940 Taliesin Way
Avery, Illinois

Used to Decorate Napkin Rings

Instructions on page 96

Tea Bag Folded Medallion

Tea Bag Folded Photo Medallion

Designed by Lani Temple

SUPPLIES

Decorative paper, 3" or 2-1/2" squares depending on size medallion desired (16 squares per medallion)

Ribbon

Hot glue sticks and glue gun

Photo to put in medallion

INSTRUCTIONS

for Making Medallion:

1. Cut 16 squares 3" or 2-1/2" (depending on size medallion desired). See Fig. 1.

2. Fold square in half diagonally; unfold. See Fig. 2.

3. Fold each side point to the center. See Fig. 3.

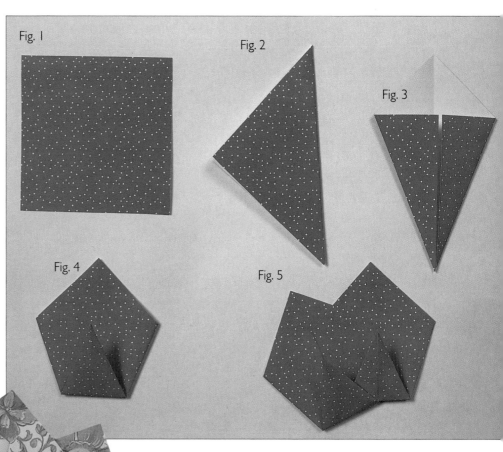

Fig. 1 Fig. 2 Fig. 3 Fig. 4 Fig. 5

4. Turn over. Fold narrow bottom point up to center of widest width. See Fig. 4.

5. Repeat steps 2 through 4 for all 16 pieces.

6. Slide right corner of one fold under left corner of adjacent folded piece so that the center fold of one piece meets with edge of the other piece. Repeat with all 16 folded pieces. Dot glue under corners to secure. See Fig. 5.

for Medallion Family Tree:

1. Make as many medallions as desired.

2. Cut a photo to fit in center circle of each medallion-frame. Tape to back of each medallion.

3. Hot-glue medallions with photos to hanging ribbon. ❑

99

Muffin Paper Frame

Designed by Patty Cox

This is called a "muffin frame" because the first one Patty Cox made, she made by folding a muffin paper. The small size frame paper piece is the same size as a muffin paper. The frame can be made of varying sizes, depending upon the size circle you start with. To use frame for a refrigerator magnet, simply glue a piece of magnetic tape to the back of frame.

SUPPLIES

Circle of paper (smaller frame is made with a 4-3/8" circle; larger frame is made with an 8-1/8" circle)
Gold metallic wax
Cotton swab
Clear acrylic spray sealer
Pressed floral
Photo magnet backing

INSTRUCTIONS

1. Cut out paper according to pattern. Lightly pencil folding lines as shown on pattern.
2. Fold two sides to center (Fig. 1).
3. Fold remaining sides to center (Fig. 2).
4. Pull up and open the corners (Fig. 3). Press flat. It will now look like Fig. 4.

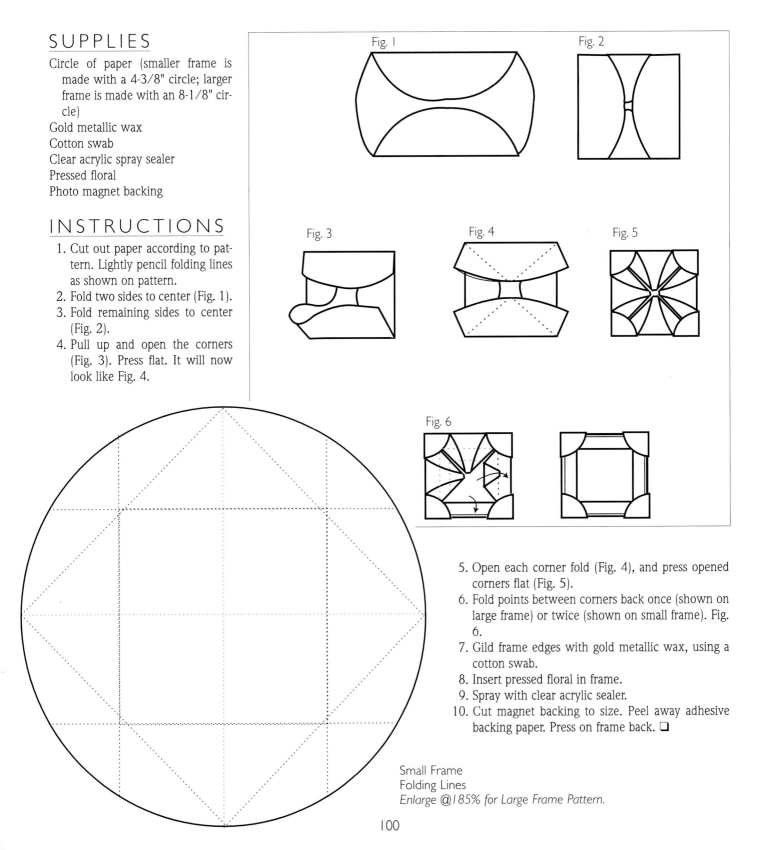

5. Open each corner fold (Fig. 4), and press opened corners flat (Fig. 5).
6. Fold points between corners back once (shown on large frame) or twice (shown on small frame). Fig. 6.
7. Gild frame edges with gold metallic wax, using a cotton swab.
8. Insert pressed floral in frame.
9. Spray with clear acrylic sealer.
10. Cut magnet backing to size. Peel away adhesive backing paper. Press on frame back. ❏

Small Frame
Folding Lines
Enlarge @185% for Large Frame Pattern.

A Victorian Frame

Designed by Patty Cox

SUPPLIES

Purple handmade paper
Thick white glue
Gold metallic wax
Lightweight cardboard
Lavender dried florals
Fancy gold button, approx. 7/8" diam.

INSTRUCTIONS

1. Cut cardboard front, back, and stand from lightweight cardboard, using patterns.
2. Cover each with purple handmade paper. Set aside to dry.
3. Cut twenty-four 2" squares from the purple paper. Fold each diagonally in half, forming a triangle. Fold in half again, forming a smaller triangle.
4. Apply gold metallic wax to sides (not base) of these small triangles, on front side only. Glue triangles overlapping each other onto the cardboard ring that is frame front. Make sure points of triangles are all going in the same direction and that front side is facing forward.
5. Glue dried florals and gold button at top of frame. (Refer to photo of project.)
6. Glue frame front to backing piece along sides and bottom, leaving top open to insert photo.
7. Glue stand on frame back. ❏

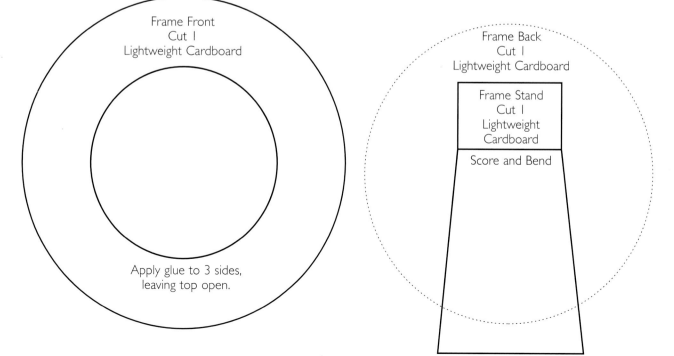

Frame Front
Cut 1
Lightweight Cardboard

Apply glue to 3 sides, leaving top open.

Frame Back
Cut 1
Lightweight Cardboard

Frame Stand
Cut 1
Lightweight Cardboard

Score and Bend

HOLIDAY MAGIC

Christmas decorating was never so wonderful ... and inexpensive! Beautiful tree ornaments, tree topper, and package decorations can be made with folded paper. Yet they look exquisite. Wreaths, stars, snowflakes – it's all here in this section.

Making your own decorations adds extra delight to the season. The projects are fun to make and beautiful to see, and there are plenty of opportunities to show them off!

Merry paper-folding Christmas to you!

A Teabag Folded Christmas Star

Designed by Lani Temple

SUPPLIES

Eight 2-1/2" squares decorative paper
Ribbon
White craft glue

INSTRUCTIONS

1. Fold square diagonally both ways; unfold. Fold in half top to bottom; unfold. See Fig. 1.

2. Fold in half diagonally (top corner down to bottom corner) to make a triangle. See Fig. 2.

3. Push left and right corners inward, making reverse folds and bringing the top corner down to form a diamond. See Fig. 3.

Fig. 1

Fig. 2

Fig. 3

Fig. 4

Fig. 5

Fig. 6

4. Each side point has two layers. Fold the right point of the top layer to center. See Fig. 4.

5. Fold the left point of top layer to center. See Fig. 5.

6. After making eight folded pieces, interlock them as follows: Slip left point of the bottom layer of one folded piece under the top layer of adjacent folded piece. Repeat with all eight folded pieces. Dot glue in folds to secure. See Fig. 6.

To hang on tree, glue a small hanging ribbon to the inside of each ornament. ❑

Christmas Wreath
GIFT CARD & NAPKIN RINGS
Designed by Patty Cox

SUPPLIES

Green handmade paper, 1/2" x 22" strip per wreath

Red raffia or ribbon bow

Thick white glue

Clear acrylic spray sealer

INSTRUCTIONS

1. Make a fold-over chain, following Figs. 1-4.

2. Glue chain ends together, forming a ring, to make the wreath. Let dry.

3. Pull chain open for a circle. Push this ring onto a small bottle lid to secure its round shape and spray with clear acrylic sealer. Remove when dry.

4. Tie a small red bow and glue on center-bottom of wreath, covering glued ends. This completes a napkin ring or a package ornament.

5. To make a gift card, follow card instructions for "Grapes On a Gift Card" project. See page 66. ❏

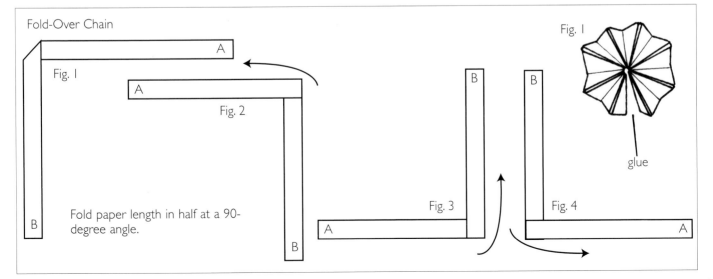

Fold-Over Chain

Fig. 1

Fig. 2

Fold paper length in half at a 90-degree angle.

Fig. 3

Fig. 4

Fig. 1

glue

A Star Tree Topper or Ornament

Designed by Patty Cox

SUPPLIES

Mottled amber handmade paper, 9" square and twelve 3-1/2" squares
White craft glue
Straight pins
Clear acrylic spray sealer

INSTRUCTIONS

1. Cut twelve 3-1/2" squares of handmade paper.
2. Fold square in half both ways and crease to find center (Fig. 1). Open folds.
3. Fold corners to center (Fig. 2).
4. Crease one triangular section (Fig. 3).
5. Fold and glue crease to inside, forming a pyramid (Fig. 4).
6. Glue pyramids together by opening a flap from inside each pyramid (Fig. 5). Consistently open the flap to the right of joined edges.
7. Glue two pyramids together by gluing flap of one pyramid to inside of adjoining pyramid (Fig. 6). Secure pyramids with straight pins until glue dries.
8. Glue six pyramids together to form the star's center (Fig. 7).
9. Glue six pyramids around the star center to form star's points as shown in the photo of a finished star.
10. Glue back of star to backing paper (9" square). Let dry. Trim edges.
11. Spray star with clear acrylic spray sealer. ❑

See photo of finished star.

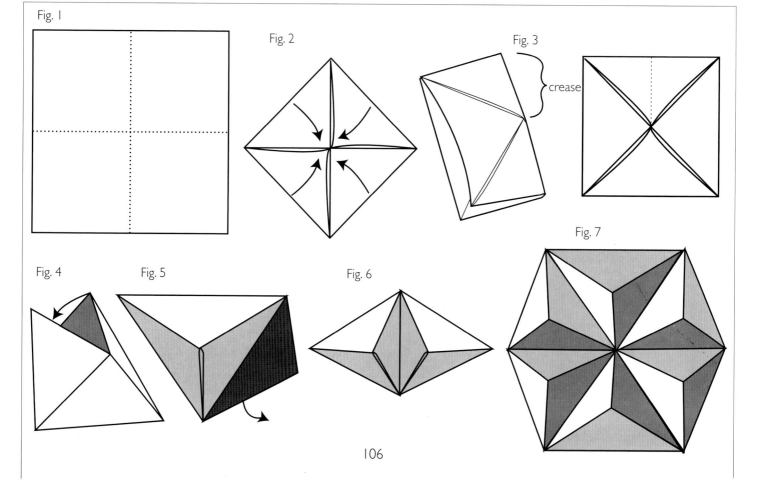

Fig. 1

Fig. 2

Fig. 3 }crease

Fig. 4

Fig. 5

Fig. 6

Fig. 7

A Victorian Ornament
Designed by Patty Cox

SUPPLIES

Twelve 2-1/2" squares burgundy mottled handmade paper

Burgundy embroidery floss, 18"

Burgundy tassel, 2"

Burgundy bead

Two gold beads

Straight pins

INSTRUCTIONS

(Refer to Figs. 1-7 with instructions for "A Star Tree Topper".)

1. Cut twelve 2" squares from the burgundy paper.

2. Follow steps 2 through 7 on page 106.

3. Glue six pyramids together to form one side of the ornament (Fig. 7).

4. Glue joined pyramids to a paper backing (same type paper) and trim away excess backing. Let dry.

5. Repeat steps to create other side of ornament.

6. Glue an embroidery floss hanging loop on top back of one half of ornament. Glue top of tassel to bottom back.

7. Glue other half of ornament to backing paper, sandwiching the loop and tassel between the two halves of ornament.

8. Thread beads on the hanging loop. ❏

A Folded Snowflake

Designed by Susan S. Mickey

SUPPLIES

Square of paper (the size will determine the size of the snowflake)

Sharp pointed scissors

Hole punch

INSTRUCTIONS

1. Fold a square of paper in half diagonally to make a triangle (Fig. 1).

2. With point of triangle upward, fold the right corner up and across (Fig. 2).

3. Fold the left corner up and across (Fig. 3).

4. Fold your shape in half as shown (Fig. 4).

5. Cut off the top as shown (Fig. 5). Keep the bottom shape.

6. Cut shapes and punch holes through all layers, cutting through folded edges and along top (Fig. 6).

7. Unfold your snowflake! This makes one flat snowflake.

8. To make a 3-dimensional snowflake, make two snowflakes of the exact same size and design. Make a slit into each snowflake, from edge of one quadrant to center. (Fig. 7) Slide slit of one snowflake into the other slit. With a small piece of transparent tape, secure end of each slit. ❑

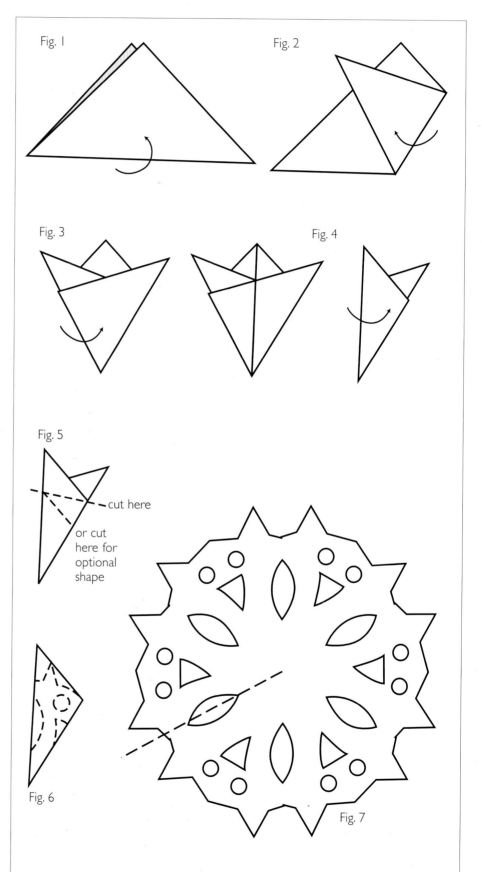

Fig. I

Fig. 2

Fig. 3

Fig. 4

Fig. 5

cut here

or cut here for optional shape

Fig. 6

Fig. 7

A Tussie Mussie Ornament

Designed by Patty Cox

SUPPLIES

Round silver doily, 4" diam.

Gold metallic wax

White tissue paper, 3" square

Gilded cedar branches

Red berries

Gold cord, 6" length

White craft glue

Low-melt glue sticks and glue gun

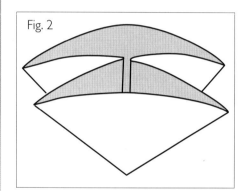

Fig. 2

INSTRUCTIONS

1. Apply gold metallic wax along outer edge of doily.
2. Fold in half both ways to find center. Unfold. Then fold in half diagonally to the previous folds as shown in Fig. 1. Crease.
3. Push each side of last fold to inside to create cone (Fig. 2). Glue these folds to inside of cone shape. Let dry.
4. Spray cones with clear acrylic sealer.
5. Glue ends of gold cord to inside edges of cone on two opposite sides.
6. Insert a 3" square of white tissue inside cone.
7. Glue cedar branches and berries into tissue paper lining. ❏

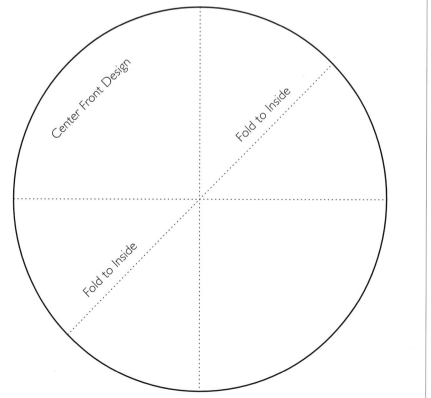

Center Front Design

Fold to Inside

Fold to Inside

METRIC CONVERSION CHART
Inches to Millimeters and Centimeters

Inches	MM	CM		Yards	Meters
1/8	3	.3		1/8	.11
1/4	6	.6		1/4	.23
3/8	10	1.0		3/8	.34
1/2	13	1.3		1/2	.46
5/8	16	1.6		5/8	.57
3/4	19	1.9		3/4	.69
7/8	22	2.2		7/8	.80
1	25	2.5		1	.91
1-1/4	32	3.2		2	1.83
1-1/2	38	3.8		3	2.74
1-3/4	44	4.4		4	3.66
2	51	5.1		5	4.57
3	76	7.6		6	5.49
4	102	10.2		7	6.40
5	127	12.7		8	7.32
6	152	15.2		9	8.23
7	178	17.8		10	9.14
8	203	20.3			
9	229	22.9			
10	254	25.4			
11	279	27.9			
12	305	30.5			

INDEX

INDEX